A Guide to
Musical Temperament

Thomas Donahue

The Scarecrow Press, Inc.
Lanham, Maryland • Toronto • Oxford
2005

VISUAL & PERFORMING ARTS

SCARECROW PRESS, INC.

Published in the United States of America
by Scarecrow Press, Inc.
A wholly owned subsidiary of
The Rowman & Littlefield Publishing Group, Inc.
4501 Forbes Boulevard, Suite 200, Lanham, Maryland 20706
www.scarecrowpress.com

PO Box 317
Oxford
OX2 9RU, UK

British Library Cataloguing in Publication Information Available

Library of Congress Cataloging-in-Publication Data
Donahue, Thomas, 1953-
  A guide to musical temperament / Thomas Donahue.
    p. cm.
  Includes bibliographical references and index.
  ISBN 0-8108-5438-4 (pbk. : alk. paper)
  1. Musical temperament. 2. Tuning. I. Title.

ML3809.D66 2005
784.192'8--dc22   2005017910

In memory of my father
John B. Donahue, Jr.
1921–2005

Contents

Foreword

Keyboard tuning deals with shapes, patterns, and relationships. On the surface it may appear to be only a set of arcane listening skills that require considerable experience, informed by hours of mathematical calculation. Those are indeed necessary. But behind it all we are dealing with fundamental symmetries and asymmetries and the dynamic processes that produce music. These relationships of organized sound are then used to build compositions and expressive performances, giving tension and resolution as the music moves along with a balanced blend of melody and harmony.

For a keyboard that has only twelve different notes within an octave, those twelve relative pitches cannot change during a performance. That is both a limitation and a strength. The tuner must find some pattern of pitch adjustments that will give good musical results in the music to be played. How does the music sound appropriately balanced and expressive? What is useful in an instrument's regular maintenance or for any particular performance?

The proper setup of the keyboard might differ from one cultural milieu to another, with an aim of reconstructing historical conditions matching the repertoire. From a practical angle, a temperament choice might favor the scales and chords to be used most often within a particular concert. A specific temperament might be requested by the other instrumentalists and singers with whom the keyboard will be played, as they will be at the mercy of the pitches produced. Some of the decisions might indeed be left to a performer's personal tastes or to the quirks of a particular instrument or acoustic space.

How is a tuner to know where to begin in all this, seeking artistically and historically appropriate layouts of the pitches for practical use? What range of possibilities is available? Which layouts are easier to set up than others under adverse conditions of time pressure or noise? How much should a tuner's ease be a determining factor in the musical results?

A tuner also eventually needs to know: How can the selection of a keyboard temperament influence other aspects of the performance process, beyond merely intonation? How may the temperament be integrated into the fundamental approach to the music, affecting the phrasing, timing, accent structure, and tempo? Can events in the intonation be important special effects built into the composition, and how may they be controlled? How do we know what the composers themselves expected or would have favored? What might the musicians learn through rehearsal and analysis, choosing a keyboard temperament *before* beginning to study the composition in other depth? These are the types of interpretive questions faced by performers and tuners.

The experience of musical study is enriched by a firm understanding of the intonational options. A performer who understands temperament, beyond merely following someone's written instructions or copying notes from a machine, will have a broader imagination and flexibility in the task of musical interpretation. The application of a temperament need not be an arbitrary or a last-minute choice, or something to leave only to the discretion of the "techies." The keyboard art may be a comprehensive package: tuning, performance, improvisation, and composition. Other instrumentalists and singers must be aware of their intonation from note to note, controlling their pitches accurately by musical and technical context, so why should it be any different for keyboard artists?

This book is a good place for a reader to begin exploring the vast field of historical keyboard tuning. It is a concise synthesis of the available literature in English. Through systematic presentation of nomenclature, calculations, and example temperaments, the author demonstrates basic tuning concepts. References are provided for those who wish to read more deeply into the literature, from the classic texts through some of the newest findings.

Another important feature here is the set of instructions to build a temperament-analysis spreadsheet on a computer. By working through this exercise the reader can gain another type of valuable practical experience. Similarly, the section of formula worksheets encourages the reader to strategize with unfamiliar temperaments. Working from a laconic description of a resulting layout found in some old or new publication, how can the seeker derive an appropriate set of practical instructions to produce that result? How can ratios, commas, or cents be translated into straightforward bearing steps? The present book describes some of those problem-solving approaches, such as looking for symmetries and for specific beat rates that will be relatively easy to hear.

There is a careful balance between practical hands-on experience at the keyboard and mathematical theory behind the pitch adjustments. The reader is encouraged not only to memorize a few favorite temperaments but also to understand some of the differences between them and to gain a working knowledge of the overall patterns. Temperaments that look unrelated on paper (for example, "Vallotti" and "Werckmeister III") may in fact be closely related, whether through historical evolution or by design. The author's practical instructions make it easy to set up various examples and to test them directly with music. He encourages the reader to *become* a tuning "techie" at an appropriate level, with the direct experience of trying it all for oneself.

In summary, this book encourages the keyboard student and enthusiast to learn not only how to follow instructions and how to approach the broader literature, but also how to think in a creative and organized manner. The point is to get an appropriate pattern of intervals installed into the keyboard confidently so that the musical ear may learn from its melodic and harmonic shapes directly in practice and experimentation. Tuning and musicianship is about the scientific process of exploring the possibilities.

Bradley Lehman
April 2005

Preface

This work is an introduction to the subject of musical temperament. While much of the material is appropriate for anyone wishing to gain an understanding of the subject, it is particularly aimed at players of stringed keyboard instruments—the harpsichord, clavichord, and forte-piano—who routinely tune their own instruments and are likely to deal with more than one temperament. The work had its inception as a twenty-page essay in *The Modern Classical Organ*. Now, as then, I have built on the foundation laid by previous authors, notably *Tuning and Temperament* by J. Murray Barbour, *The Acoustical Foundations of Music* by John Backus, *Unequal Temperaments and Their Role in the Performance of Early Music* by Claudio Di Veroli, *Tuning the Historical Temperaments by Ear* by Owen Jorgensen, and the numerous writings of Mark Lindley.

There are three main premises of this book. First, one should have a firm grounding in the theoretical basis for temperament, which includes a familiarity with the mathematics involved. This greatly enhances the process of understanding and also helps to untangle the myriad of seemingly conflicting material written about temperament. Second, there needs to be a presentation of the practical aspects of temperament for performers, which includes the musical ramifications and how temperaments may be set on musical instruments. Third, one should be familiar with the historical aspects of the subject in order to help relate a specific temperament with a particular musical work and to gain an appreciation of the differences of opinion on the subject.

Rather than address each of these three areas individually, the first part of the book intertwines them in a progressive discussion. Chapter 1 has three sections. The first section presents several preliminary topics that need to be understood before describing the need for temperament: frequency, frequency ratios, cents, the circle of fifths, and fixed intonation. The second section details the tuning discrepancies that create the need for temperament and gives the general solution to the problem. The third section discusses the harmonic series and beats, topics which offer the first connection of theory with practice. Chapter 2 presents sixteen representative temperaments that illustrate different concrete approaches to the tuning discrepancies described in chapter 1. Chapter 3 discusses the musical implications of three representative temperaments in terms of their major thirds, semitones, and key signatures. Chapter 4 correlates theory and practice by presenting a method of creating instructions for setting a temperament that are derived from the representations given in chapter 2. Chapter 5 reviews the procedures and skills needed to set a temperament on a stringed keyboard instrument. Chapter 6 presents tuning instructions based on the method given in chapter 4 for the sixteen representative temperaments. Chapter 7 reviews the historical aspects of the main categories of temperament, touching on the subject of temperament selection as well as the question of temperament and the music of J. S. Bach. As a further assistance to the reader in clarifying contradictory or confusing material, specific sources of confusion are addressed in several chapters.

The second part of the book is more reference related, devoted to supplementary topics such as pitch references, starting notes, comparison of different versions of temperaments, near-equal temperaments, advanced calculations, addition temperament data, the use of spreadsheets, and instructions in a musical notation format.

The designations or "spellings" of notes used here are C, C♯, D, E♭, E, F, F♯, G, G♯, A, B♭, and B. It must be admitted that these note names will result in having some intervals "misspelled" some of the time, such as B–E♭ instead of B–D♯. This is an aspect that simply must be accepted, since alternatives are no better. The use of "D♯/E♭" as a single-note designation is needlessly complicated, which leads to even more convoluted interval spelling such as "D♯/E♭–A♯/B♭."

The pitch designations used here for each octave of a keyboard instrument are CC, C, c, c^1, c^2, and c^3, with c^1 being "middle C" and c being "tenor C," one octave lower. Italics are used when referring to actual pitches; this helps to distinguish between the use of superscripts for both pitches and endnotes, and also differentiates the pitch "a" from the indefinite article "a." When referring to a note in a general way—such as, "One may set a temperament by starting on either an A or a C"—an uppercase, non-italic typeface will be used.

Part 1
Main Material

1

The Basis for Temperament

Preliminary Topics

In preparation for explaining what *temperament* is, several topics will be presented that serve as the groundwork for the discussion to follow. The topics include frequency, frequency ratios, cents, the circle of fifths, and fixed intonation. Complete discussions of these topics may be found in books on acoustics[1] and in music dictionaries.[2]

Frequency

Musical sound begins as vibration; an example is the back-and-forth motion of a plucked harpsichord string. These vibrations are periodic, meaning they have a regular pattern like the movement of a clock pendulum. These periodic vibrations disturb the surrounding air so that it too develops a similar pattern. This is a sound wave. A sound wave is not like the back-and-forth vibrations of the string; rather, it is the motion of air molecules being pushed closer together then further apart, a compression and an expansion. The sound wave pattern exactly matches the original vibration pattern. Each pair of back-and-forth or compression-and-expansion is referred to as one cycle, and it is the number of cycles that go by in one second, how frequently the cycle repeats, that interests us. This is the *frequency* of the sound. Frequencies are useful because they can be measured. Related to frequency is *pitch*, which is our subjective experience of frequency. Roughly, when the number of cycles per second is greater, the frequency is greater, and we say the musical tone has a higher pitch compared to another tone with fewer cycles per second and a lower frequency.

On the modern piano, the strings representing the A above middle C—having the designation a^I—are put under enough tension so they vibrate at a frequency of 440 cycles per second. The term "cycles per second" has come to be called "Hertz" after the nineteenth-century German physicist Heinrich Hertz, and is abbreviated Hz. So, it is said that the frequency of a^1 = 440 Hz.

A brief mention should be made about terminology. The word "tone" is usually used when the discussion centers on acoustics or the physics of sound, while the word "note" is more often used in a musical context. This will be the usage employed here. However, there may be instances in which the two words are interchangeable. (Some writers use the word "note" in the very strict sense of signifying the notation symbols placed on a staff; that is, half note, quarter note, eighth note, and so on.)

Frequency Ratios

An *interval* is the relationship between two notes; of particular interest to us is when two notes are played simultaneously. We can characterize an interval in two ways. First, it may be given a name based on the relationship between the two notes in a diatonic scale, the type of scale that results from playing the natural keys on the piano from C to C. For example, starting at middle C or c^1, the next highest pitch with the same letter name is c^2, and the interval c^1–c^2 is called an *octave*. This term is derived from the Latin word for "eight" and refers to the fact that the interval includes the first and eighth notes of the diatonic scale

$$c^1\ d^1\ e^1\ f^1\ g^1\ a^1\ b^1\ c^2.$$

Second, an interval may be characterized by the relationship of the frequencies of its two notes. The frequency of the higher note in the octave interval is twice that of the lower note, so one may say the octave has a frequency ratio of 2 to 1, usually written 2:1. This ratio holds true regardless of the actual frequencies. Whether two notes have frequencies of 100 and 200 Hz, or 262 and 524 Hz, each pair of notes has a frequency ratio of 2:1 and may be called an octave.

The six main intervals we will be dealing with are given in table 1.1. The frequency ratios are given in column 2, and their decimal equivalents are given in column 3. Both the frequency ratio and its decimal equivalent are given because each will prove to be useful in its

Table 1.1. Numerical Characterizations of Pure Intervals

Interval	Freq. Ratio	Decimal	Cents
perfect octave	2:1	2.00	1200
perfect fifth	3:2	1.50	702
perfect fourth	4:3	1.33 ...	498
major third	5:4	1.25	386
minor third	6:5	1.20	316
major sixth	5:3	1.66 ...	884

own way. The one qualification that should be made is that these ratios refer to intervals that are tuned pure. This will be explained in more detail later. (Some people use the word "just" as a synonym for "pure.")

Cents

Some of the frequency ratios we will encounter cannot be represented with simple whole numbers as those in table 1.1. In order to avoid complicated numbers, frequency ratios may be converted to a different number that will simplify matters. This involves the concept of *cents*, which was devised by Alexander Ellis in the late nineteenth century and is based on the logarithm of an interval's frequency ratio. The relationship is

cent value = 3986 × log (frequency ratio).

The resulting number is a single value that may be understood as the size of the interval. The derivation of this equation is given in chapter 11. The equation is easy to use with the help of a scientific calculator with a logarithm key: take the logarithm of the decimal equivalent of the frequency ratio and multiply the result by 3986. For the interval of an octave the calculation is

octave cent value = 3986 × log (2.0) = 1200.

Thus, the octave, with a frequency ratio of 2:1, has a value of 1200 cents. The cent values of the main intervals are given in table 1.1, column 4, rounded to the nearest cent. Once we begin discussing non-pure intervals, the simple 3:2 or 5:4 ratios will not apply, and we will switch to cent values to make calculations easier.

Since the present discussion will only be referring to octaves, fifths, and fourths that are perfect—as opposed to augmented and diminished—the designation "perfect" will be dropped for these intervals.

Circle of Fifths

There are twelve notes in the chromatic scale. In ascending order they are C, C♯, D, E♭, E, F, F♯, G, G♯, A, B♭, and B. For our purposes, a different order is used, because this will make it easier to describe what temperament is. The alternate order is such that adjacent note names describe the interval of a fifth: C, G, D, A, E, B, F♯, C♯, G♯, E♭, B♭, and F. This arrangement is referred to as the *circle of fifths* because C—which forms a fifth with F—can be made to follow F when the notes are arranged in a circle. This concept was first described in 1728 by Johann David Heinichen.

Fixed Intonation

Intonation usually refers to the ability to produce a given pitch accurately. We will define it as the capacity of a musical instrument to allow a performer to adjust the pitch of an instrument while performing. An instrument with *flexible intonation* allows such adjustments; a low degree of flexible intonation is possible with woodwinds instruments, and a high degree of flexible intonation is possible with bowed string instruments and the human voice. On the other hand, instruments with *fixed intonation* have their pitches preset and non-adjustable as one performs. This is a characteristic of keyboard instruments: harpsichord, clavichord, piano, and pipe organ. (The clavichord actually does allow the performer a small pitch-adjustment capability, but this is usually used only for a vibrato effect.) We will be concentrating on instruments with fixed intonation, particularly the stringed keyboard instruments.

Temperament Explained

With the preliminary topics presented, we can now explain the tuning discrepancies that create the need for temperament and how we may deal with those discrepancies.

Tuning Discrepancies

If we start on the note C and tune a series of twelve pure fifths, we end up eventually at c^6, seven octaves higher than where we started; that is, $C-G$, $G-d$, $d-a$, $a-e^1$, e^1-b^1, $b^1-f\#^2$, $f\#^2-c\#^3$, $c\#^3-g\#^3$, $g\#^3-eb^4$, eb^4-bb^4, bb^4-f^5, and f^5-c^6. Then, if we start on the same note C as before and tune seven consecutive pure octaves, we theoretically end up on the same note c^6 again; that is, $C-c$, $c-c^1$, c^1-c^2, c^2-c^3, c^3-c^4, c^4-c^5, and c^5-c^6. However, the two ending notes do not coincide. The note reached through twelve pure fifth intervals has a higher frequency than the note reached through seven pure octave intervals.

This can be illustrated mathematically. We start with a hypothetical frequency for C of 65.5 Hz, and the frequency ratio of a pure fifth, 1.5. Tuning twelve pure fifths from this frequency means multiplying 65.5 by 1.5 twelve times, or

$$65.5 \times (1.5)^{12} = 8498.4 \text{ Hz.}$$

Tuning seven pure octaves means multiplying 65.5 by 2.0 seven times, or

$$65.5 \times (2.0)^7 = 8384.0 \text{ Hz.}$$

Notice the discrepancy. Rather than dealing with these numbers as a frequency ratio, we can simplify the calculations using cents. A pure fifth is 702 cents, and a pure octave is 1200 cents. The cent value of twelve fifths is

$$12 \times 702 = 8424 \text{ cents.}$$

The cent value of seven octaves is

$$7 \times 1200 = 8400 \text{ cents.}$$

The difference is

$$8424 - 8400 = 24 \text{ cents.}$$

This 24-cent discrepancy between twelve pure fifths and seven pure octaves is called the *Pythagorean comma* or *ditonic comma*. (See chapter 4 for a discussion of rounded vs. precise values for this and other numbers.)

Another discrepancy exists. If we start on c and tune four pure fifths—c–g, g–d^l, d^l–a^l, and a^l–e^2—then lower e^2 by two octaves, the interval c–e thus formed is a major third. However, it is not a pure major third with a frequency ratio of 5:4 and a value of 386 cents (table 1.1); it has a larger frequency ratio and a higher cent value. Mathematically, the cent value of four pure fifth intervals is

$$4 \times 702 = 2808 \text{ cents.}$$

Dropping down two octaves means subtracting 1200 cents twice, or

$$2808 - 1200 - 1200 = 408 \text{ cents.}$$

This is the size of the wide major third. A pure major third has a value of 386 cents, so the difference is

$$408 - 386 = 22 \text{ cents.}$$

This 22-cent discrepancy is called the *syntonic comma*. The difference between the Pythagorean comma and the syntonic comma is two cents, and is known as the *schisma*.

Other tuning discrepancies exist, but they do not directly affect the present discussion.

The fact that the size of any major third is dependent on the sizes of four consecutive fifth intervals in the circle of fifths is an important point to which we will return.

General Solution

The problem may now be stated this way: the existence of the Pythagorean comma tells us that pure octaves and pure fifths cannot co-exist on instruments with fixed intonation. On a keyboard instrument, if one tunes the octaves pure, the twelve fifths cannot be pure, and vice versa.

To solve this problem, one tunes the octaves pure and then adjusts some or all of the twelve fifth intervals so that their frequency ratios are slightly less than 3:2 and their cent values are slightly less than 702 cents. One does this until the total cent value of the adjusted fifths is 24 cents less than twelve pure fifths. In other words, the cent values of all twelve fifth intervals in the circle of fifths cannot add up to 8424 cents; they can only add up to 8400 cents. The different ways that have been devised to remove the value of the Pythagorean comma from the circle of fifths will be presented in chapter 2.

In actual practice, adjusting any given fifth interval in the circle of fifths means lowering the pitch of the higher note or raising the pitch of the lower note. The interval is then said to be "narrower than pure." Generally, adjusted fifths are narrower than pure, and adjusted fourths and major thirds are wider than pure; there are exceptions, which will be mentioned later. It should also be noted that not all intervals need to be adjusted; some fifths, fourths, and major thirds may remain pure.

The ultimate mathematical goal of this adjustment process is to remove 24 cents from the circle of fifths. The ultimate musical goal is to adjust the sizes of the fifths—after 24 cents is removed—in such a way that the intervals that are considered important are given priority. For example, major thirds are a fundamental element of harmony, and since the size of any major third is governed by the sizes of four consecutive fifth intervals, one must also adjust the fifths to regulate the sizes of the major thirds. This is discussed in chapter 3.

The process of adjusting the size of an interval by making it narrower or wider than pure is called *tempering*. Any plan that describes the adjustments to the sizes of some or all of the twelve fifth intervals in the circle of fifths so that they accommodate pure octaves and produce certain sizes of major thirds is called a *temperament*.

One almost universal priority is that the octaves have to remain pure. Luckily, the fifths and major thirds need not be pure, and the amount of tempering that needs to be done generally is not enough to make the tempered intervals sound out of tune. However, some intervals in some temperaments may sound objectionable, and in certain instances selected intervals are "sacrificed" and end up being musically unusable. The reason why our ears can tolerate tempered fifths and thirds will be discussed below.

Manifestation of Temperament

Two subjects are now presented that relate the theoretical necessity for temperament to a practical, audible means of tuning musical instruments.

Harmonic Series

A characteristic of a sound produced by a musical instrument is its *timbre*, sometimes called *tone color*. This is the quality of the sound that lets us distinguish a piano from a harpsichord or a violin, even when notes of the same pitch and loudness are played. The primary basis for timbre is the fact that a sound is made up of many partial sounds that coalesce. A specific timbre is the result of how many partial sounds there are and of each partial sound's relative strength or prominence.

In a musical sound we concentrate on those partial sounds that have a regular pattern to them—that is, that have a frequency—as opposed to a partial sound with an irregular pattern, which is noise. The lowest partial sound with a frequency corresponds to the note being played and is called the *fundamental frequency* or *first harmonic frequency*. In addition to the fundamental frequency, other frequencies are present that contribute to the timbre of the total sound. These *upper harmonic frequencies* are related to the fundamental frequency in a very specific way. For example, the second harmonic frequency has a frequency twice that of the fundamental frequency. Similarly, the third harmonic frequency has a frequency three times that of the fundamental frequency. In general terms, the frequency of the nth harmonic frequency is n times the fundamental frequency. The collection of fundamental frequency and upper harmonic frequencies that are related by whole numbers is called the *harmonic series*.

Neighboring harmonic frequencies in the harmonic series are related to each other by the common music intervals; that is, the second harmonic frequency is an octave above the fundamental frequency (hence the ratio 2:1); the third harmonic frequency is a fifth above the second (hence the ratio 3:2); and so on. The first six harmonic frequencies and their relationships are given in table 1.2. Even though notes and approximate frequencies are given in the last column, this is only for illustrative purposes. It should be understood that all the frequencies

Table 1.2. Relationships in the Harmonic Series

Harmonic Frequency	Is above the	By the Interval of a(n)	Whose Freq. Ratio Is	Example
6th	5th	minor third	6:5	g^2 (786 Hz or 6f)
5th	4th	major third	5:4	e^2 (655 Hz or 5f)
4th	3rd	fourth	4:3	c^2 (524 Hz or 4f)
3rd	2nd	fifth	3:2	g^1 (393 Hz or 3f)
2nd	1st	octave	2:1	c^1 (262 Hz or 2f)
1st	—	—	—	c (131 Hz or f)

coalesce into a single complex sound, and we characterize that sound by the note name and frequency of its fundamental frequency. The importance of the location of the pitches of the upper harmonic frequencies listed in the last column will be discussed later.

Beats

The term "pure" has been mentioned several times to describe intervals with simple frequency ratios such as 3:2 and 5:4. Now we will discuss what this means in relation to tempered intervals. The difference between a pure interval and a tempered interval can actually be heard, and this gives us a way to set each type of interval on a musical instrument.

Every musical note is a complex sound that is made up of a fundamental frequency and several upper harmonic frequencies. For a single note, all the upper harmonic frequencies form pure, "in-tune" relationships with the fundamental frequency. When two notes are sounded together, two harmonic series are superimposed, and certain upper harmonic frequencies are the same or nearly the same. These frequencies are called *coinciding harmonic frequencies* and can be determined from the frequency ratio of the interval involved.

Let us take the example of a pure fifth interval. If we start with the note c with a hypothetical frequency of 131.0 Hz, the note g that forms a pure fifth with c has a frequency of 196.5 Hz. This is calculated by multiplying the frequency of c by the frequency ratio of the fifth, which is 3:2 or 1.5; that is, 131.0 × 1.5 = 196.5. Now we calculate the upper

harmonic frequencies for each note by multiplying each fundamental
frequency by 2, 3, 4, and so on. The results are shown in table 1.3.

Table 1.3. Harmonic Frequencies of the Pure Fifth *c–g* (3:2)

No.	Harmonic Frequencies		Relationship
6th	786.0 Hz	1179.0 Hz	6f
5th	655.0	982.5	5f
4th	524.0	786.0	4f
3rd	**393.0**	589.5	3f
2nd	262.0	**393.0**	2f
1st	131.0 (*c*)	196.5 (*g*)	f

The fundamental frequencies of the two notes *c* and *g* are in the
bottom row: 131.0 Hz and 196.5 Hz respectively. Each set of numbers
in columns 2 and 3 represent the harmonic series of each note related
by the sequence f, 2f, 3f, 4f, and so on, which is indicated in column 4.
Notice that the *third* harmonic frequency of *c* and the *second* harmonic
frequency of *g* have the same value: 393.0 Hz, shown in bold type;
these are the coinciding harmonic frequencies. Notice also that their
number names—three and two—correspond to the frequency ratio of
the fifth, 3:2.

The harmonic frequencies of other intervals are given in table 1.4.
Again, the frequency ratio that identifies each interval also identifies
the upper harmonic frequencies that coincide for that interval. Since the
fundamental frequencies are based on pure intervals, the coinciding
frequencies for these particular intervals are exactly the same value.

Now consider a pure fifth and a tempered fifth (table 1.5). The
pure fifth has the same fundamental frequencies as above, 131.0 and
196.5 Hz. The tempered fifth has its *g* frequency lowered slightly to
195.8 Hz, making that fifth narrower than pure. Since the fundamental
frequency of *g* in the tempered fifth is slightly lower than the fundamental frequency of *g* in the pure fifth, the upper harmonic frequencies
of the note *g* in the tempered fifth are also correspondingly lower. As a
result, the coinciding harmonic frequencies in the tempered fifth are not
the same value; they are now 393.0 and 391.7 Hz.

Table 1.4. Harmonic Frequencies of Selected Intervals

No.	Fourth (4:3)		Major Third (5:4)	
6th	786.0 Hz	1048.0 Hz	786.0 Hz	982.5 Hz
5th	655.0	873.3	**655.0**	818.8
4th	**524.0**	698.7	524.0	**655.0**
3rd	393.0	**524.0**	393.0	491.3
2nd	262.0	349.3	262.0	327.5
1st	131.0 (c)	174.7 (f)	131.0 (c)	163.8 (e)

No.	Minor Third (6:5)		Major Sixth (5:3)	
6th	**786.0** Hz	943.2 Hz	786.0 Hz	1310.0 Hz
5th	655.0	**786.0**	**655.0**	1091.7
4th	524.0	628.8	524.0	873.3
3rd	393.0	471.6	393.0	**655.0**
2nd	262.0	314.4	262.0	436.7
1st	131.0 (c)	157.2 (e♭)	131.0 (c)	218.3 (a)

Table 1.5. Harmonic Frequencies of a Pure and a Tempered Fifth

No.	Pure Fifth		Tempered Fifth	
6th	786.0 Hz	1179.0 Hz	786.0 Hz	1175.0 Hz
5th	655.0	982.5	655.0	979.2
4th	524.0	786.0	524.0	783.3
3rd	**393.0**	589.5	**393.0**	587.5
2nd	262.0	**393.0**	262.0	**391.7**
1st	131.0 (c)	196.5 (g)	131.0 (c)	195.8 (g)

The difference in the coinciding harmonic frequencies of the tempered fifth can actually be heard if one were to play this interval. What one would hear is a wavering or fluctuation in the sound superimposed on the actual musical notes, and the number of fluctuations per second is the difference between the two coinciding harmonic frequencies. In this case, the difference is 391.7 − 393.0 = −1.3. (This calculation is done in such a way that the negative sign indicates the tempered interval is narrower than pure; see chapter 4.) These fluctuations are called *beats*. Beats are an important sound clue in two ways: their absence allows one to know when an interval is pure, and their presence indicates the amount of tempering of an interval. Tempered intervals beat, pure intervals do not, and the *beat rate*—the number of beats per second—is directly related to the degree of tempering.

The term "coinciding harmonic frequencies" does not refer to the fact that the frequencies are the same, because, in the example of the tempered fifth in table 1.5, they are not the same. Rather, the term refers to the harmonic frequencies—one from each note in the interval—whose number-names are related to the frequency ratio of that interval.

It should be emphasized that the "vertical" relationship of the frequencies does *not* change; the upper harmonic frequencies exhibit pure, in-tune relationships with the fundamental frequency according to the progression f, 2f, 3f, 4f, and so on, regardless of whether the interval is pure or tempered.

Because the number of beats per second is based on the difference between actual frequencies, this means that the beat rate of the same tempered fifth played an octave higher would be twice as fast. Table 1.6 gives an example of two tempered fifths an octave apart. (The beat rate of the higher interval is not exactly twice as much because the frequencies have been rounded to one decimal place.)

It was mentioned above that, while octaves need to be pure, fifths and thirds need not be. In other words, our ears can tolerate tempered fifths and thirds. The reason has to do with the strength of the upper harmonic frequencies. Generally, the lower the harmonic frequency, the stronger it tends to be. An interval with smaller numbers, such as an octave with a 2:1 frequency ratio, has coinciding harmonic frequencies that are more easily heard compared to a minor third with a 6:5 frequency ratio. The stronger, lower-numbered harmonic frequencies make beats more noticeable. The beats of a tempered octave are quite pronounced, the beats of a tempered fourth are less so, and the beats of a tempered minor third even less so. Our ears are more forgiving as the numbers in the frequency ratio increase.

There are two aspects about the location and strength of coinciding harmonic frequencies that have a direct impact on the practical side of setting a temperament on a musical instrument. First, it is easier to tune octaves and fifths than it is to tune minor thirds, because the coinciding

Table 1.6. Harmonic Frequencies of Tempered Fifths an Octave Apart

No.	c–g		c^{l}–g^{l}	
6th	786.0	1175.0	1572.0	2350.0
5th	655.0	979.2	1310.0	1958.3
4th	524.0	783.3	1048.0	1566.7
3rd	**393.0**	587.5	**786.0**	1175.0
2nd	262.0	**391.7**	524.0	**783.3**
1st	131.0 (c)	195.8 (g)	262.0 (c^{l})	391.7 (g^{l})
Beats:	$391.7 - 393.0 = -1.3$		$783.3 - 786.0 = -2.7$	

harmonic frequencies for octaves and fifths are easier to hear. Second, when one listens for beats, one needs to concentrate on the approximate pitch location where they occur. This is discussed in chapter 5.

Sources of Confusion

Terminology

Sometimes the term "overtone" is used to refer to any partial sound above the fundamental frequency. Unfortunately, this term may cause some confusion, because the first overtone is the second harmonic frequency and the second overtone is the third harmonic frequency. Since the number of each upper harmonic frequency is the same as the multiplying factor for its frequency above the fundamental frequency—that is, since the nth harmonic frequency is n times the fundamental frequency—this nomenclature is less confusing. It is recommended that "overtone" not be used as a synonym for "upper harmonic frequency."

Many people shorten the phrase "fundamental frequency" to "fundamental" and "harmonic frequency" to "harmonic." While grammatically incorrect—"fundamental" and "harmonic" are adjectives, not nouns, and should not stand by themselves—it is a fairly ingrained usage in the literature.

The word "partial" should also not be used as a synonym for a harmonic frequency. Not only is it a stand-alone adjective, but a partial sound refers to any component of a complex sound that may or may not have a frequency. In others words, it can refer to noise.

Imprecision

One of the problems in dealing with temperament calculations is that most of the numbers we will encounter are not whole numbers. For example: the value of 3986 in the cent equation is more precisely 3986.3137 (see chapter 11), and sometimes 4000 is used; the cent value for the interval of a pure fifth is more precisely 701.9550 instead of 702 cents; and several values may be used for the Pythagorean comma: 23.46, 23.5, or 24 cents (see chapter 4). We can use these more accurate values, but eventually we need to round up numbers, and we will end up with situations in which some imprecision is introduced. This accounts for the slightly different values one finds among the writings about temperament. This is an unavoidable fact with temperament calculations.

Frequency Ratios vs. Beat Rates

Frequency ratios are independent of the actual frequencies. Cent values are also independent of the actual frequencies because they are derived from frequency ratios. Beat rates are dependent on and directly related to frequencies. So, for any given interval, the same interval an octave higher would have the same frequency ratio and cent value as the lower interval, but the beat rate of the higher interval would be faster.

Number Order in Frequency Ratios

Some references to frequency ratios reverse the number order, using, for example, 2:3 instead of 3:2 for a fifth. The 2:3 order is based on arranging the fundamental frequencies from lowest to highest pitch; for the fifth c–g this would be 131.0:196.5 Hz. The convention in this book is to use 3:2 for three reasons. First, it puts the numbers in the same order as the division needed to obtain the decimal equivalent; that is, $3 \div 2 = 1.5$. Second, it produces the decimal equivalent that is the multiplier for calculating frequencies around the circle of fifths in the order C, G, D, A, E, and so on. That is, the frequency of any C multiplied by

1.5 produces the frequency of the G above that C; the frequency of any G multiplied by 1.5 produces the frequency of D above that G; and so on. Third, it identifies the coinciding harmonic frequencies in the same order as the interval designation c–g; that is, the third harmonic frequency of the lower note c and the second harmonic frequency of the higher note g.

Notation of Twelve Pure Fifths

The notation to indicate the tuning of twelve pure fifths when describing the Pythagorean comma is sometimes given as C–G, G–d, d–a, a–e^1, e^1–b^1, b^1–$f\#^2$, $f\#^2$–$c\#^3$, $c\#^3$–$g\#^3$, $g\#^3$–$d\#^4$, $d\#^4$–$a\#^4$, $a\#^4$–$e\#^5$, and $e\#^5$–$b\#^6$. This method emphasizes the discrepancy in the starting and ending notes as the difference between a C and a B$\#$.

Tempered Intervals vs. Harmonic Series

A tempered interval is one that is either wider or narrower than pure so that its two notes do not produce a simple frequency ratio. However, regardless of the relationship of the two notes to each other, the upper harmonic frequencies of *each note* form pure, in-tune relationships with that note's fundamental frequency according to the sequence f, 2f, 3f, 4f, and so on.

Inharmonicity

There is a qualification to two statements made above: that pure octaves are an almost universal priority, and that the frequencies in the harmonic series exhibit the sequence f, 2f, 3f, 4f, and so on. There are situations in which the upper harmonic frequencies are not exact whole-number multiples of the fundamental frequency. This is known as *inharmonicity*. It is of greatest importance in terms of the extreme ranges of the compass on the piano. The consequence of inharmonicity is that when a piano is tuned, the octaves in the treble tend to be wider than pure, and octaves in the bass tend to be narrower than pure. In other words, the treble notes above about c^3 are "sharp," and the bass notes below about C are "flat." This is often referred to as a "stretched" tuning.

Summary

Musical sound starts as periodic vibrations that compress and expand the air to form a sound wave. Each pair of compression-and-expansion is one cycle, and the number of cycles in one second is the frequency of the musical tone. Another name for "cycles per second" is Hertz.

An interval is the relationship of two notes. An interval may be characterized either by the distance between the notes in a diatonic scale or by the ratio of the two fundamental frequencies. Frequency ratios are independent of the actual frequencies.

Cents are an alternate way of characterizing the size of intervals, based on the logarithm of the frequency ratio. The equation is

$$\text{cent value} = 3986 \times \log (\text{frequency ratio}).$$

The advantage to cents is that complex frequency ratios are avoided and calculations are easier.

The circle of fifths is an arrangement of the twelve notes of the chromatic scale according to fifth intervals: C, G, D, A, E, B, F♯, C♯, G♯, E♭, B♭, and F. The next note in the series would be C again, giving the impression of a circular progression.

Fixed intonation is the characteristic of keyboard instruments that does not allow adjustment of the pitch of the notes as one performs.

The Pythagorean comma is the difference between twelve pure fifths and seven pure octaves. Its approximate value is 24 cents. The syntonic comma is the difference between a pure major third and a major third derived from four pure fifths. Its approximate value is 22 cents. The difference between the Pythagorean and syntonic commas is 2 cents and is called the schisma.

The size of any major third is dependent on the sizes of four consecutive fifth intervals in the circle of fifths.

Pure fifths and pure octaves cannot co-exist on musical instruments with fixed intonation. The general solution is to leave octaves pure and adjust the sizes of the fifths so that the total cent value of twelve fifths equals the total cent value of seven octaves, which is 8400 cents. In other words, it is necessary to remove the 24-cent value of the Pythagorean comma from the circle of fifths. Then the sizes of the fifths are adjusted to vary the sizes of the major thirds as needed or preferred.

Tempering is the process of altering the size of an interval by making it narrower or wider than pure. A temperament is any plan that describes the adjustments to the sizes of some or all of the twelve fifth intervals in the circle of fifths so that they accommodate pure octaves and produce certain sizes of major thirds.

A musical tone is a complex sound made up of many partial sounds. It is the number and strength of these partial sounds that determine the timbre.

The fundamental frequency of a musical tone is the lowest partial sound that has periodic vibrations. It corresponds to the note being played. The upper harmonic frequencies of a musical tone are partial sounds whose frequencies are related to the fundamental frequency by whole numbers. The harmonic series is the collection of all harmonic frequencies related in this way.

When an interval is tempered, certain upper harmonic frequencies interact; these are called coinciding harmonic frequencies. The result is beats. Beats are a regular wavering sound superimposed on the sound of the two notes of the interval. The beat rate—the number of beats per second—is the difference in the frequencies of the coinciding harmonic frequencies. The beat rate is an indication of the degree to which an interval is tempered.

Because the lower-numbered harmonic frequencies tend to be stronger, our ears are more tolerant of non-pure thirds compared to non-pure octaves. For the same reason, it is easier to tune octaves and fifths than minor thirds.

Notes

1. John Backus, *The Acoustical Foundations of Music*, 2nd ed. (New York: W. W. Norton & Company, 1977).

2. Don Michael Randel, ed., *The New Harvard Dictionary of Music* (Cambridge, Mass.: The Belknap Press of Harvard University Press, 1986); and Stanley Sadie, ed., *The New Grove Dictionary of Musical Instruments*, 3 vols., (London: Macmillan Press, 1984).

2

Selected Temperaments

The general solution for dealing with the tuning discrepancy between pure fifths and pure octaves is to remove the value of the Pythagorean comma from the circle of fifths. We now examine how this is specifically done for selected temperaments. In order to understand the characteristics of each temperament and to be able to compare and contrast them, the information about the fifths will be given in three different ways. In the tables that follow, the first column gives the note names that comprise the fifth intervals. The second column gives a shorthand version of the tempering; these terms are explained with each temperament or are self-explanatory. The third column lists the cent values of the fifths; this column adds up to 8400 cents, which is the seven-octave restriction mentioned in chapter 1. The fourth column shows how the Pythagorean comma was removed from the circle of fifths; this column adds up to −24 cents. The cent values of the major thirds are also listed for completeness; they are calculated by adding the cent values of the four constituent fifths and subtracting 2400. Major thirds will be discussed more thoroughly in chapter 3.

Pythagorean tuning (table 2.1) is characterized by eleven pure fifths. The twelfth interval cannot be pure because of the necessity of removing 24 cents from the circle of fifths, so it is narrower than pure by the entire Pythagorean comma (abbreviated "−1 PC"). This is the interval that is sacrificed and, depending on the exact musical requirements, could be placed anywhere in the circle of fifths. Strictly speaking, Pythagorean tuning is not a temperament because one does not temper any intervals; one simply tunes eleven pure fifths and accepts the interval that is left over. (This distinction brings up a point of terminology. The convention used here is that one *tunes* pure intervals but *tempers* an interval wider or narrower than pure.)

This tuning is good for exploring plainchant, organum, and gothic

21

Table 2.1. Pythagorean Tuning

	Fifths			Major Thirds	
Interval	Tempering	Cents	Comma	Interval	Cents
C–G	pure	702	0	C–E	408
G–D	pure	702	0	G–B	408
D–A	pure	702	0	D–F♯	408
A–E	pure	702	0	A–C♯	408
E–B	pure	702	0	E–G♯	408
B–F♯	pure	702	0	B–E♭	384
F♯–C♯	pure	702	0	F♯–B♭	384
C♯–G♯	pure	702	0	C♯–F	384
G♯–E♭	–1 PC	678	–24	G♯–C	384
E♭–B♭	pure	702	0	E♭–G	408
B♭–F	pure	702	0	B♭–D	408
F–C	pure	702	0	F–A	408

polyphony at the keyboard.[1] Its characteristic major third of 408 cents—often referred to as a Pythagorean third—was not used as a stable element in chords. Rather, it was used as an element of tension leading to a pure fifth. A typical cadence in thirteenth- and fourteenth-century music was $g–b–e^l \rightarrow f–c^l–f^l$, in which the third $g–b$ resolves to the fifth $f–c^l$ and the sixth $g–e^l$ resolves to the octave $f–f^l$. This progression may seem strange but makes sense with Pythagorean tuning.[2]

Notice that a Pythagorean third appears wherever there are four consecutive pure fifths; for example, the third B♭–D is derived from the fifths B♭–F, F–C, C–G, and G–D. This type of third will show up in other temperaments to be discussed later.

Table 2.2 shows 1/4-comma meantone temperament, described by Bartolomeo Ramos de Pareja in 1482 and by Pietro Aaron in 1523.[3] Its characteristic feature is eight pure major thirds. It is a temperament that was used at a time when thirds were an important musical element. As mentioned previously, four consecutive pure fifths produce a Pythagorean major third that is 408 cents. Since a pure major third is 386 cents, four pure fifths form a major third that is wider than pure by the syntonic comma, or 22 cents. In 1/4-comma meantone temperament, each

Table 2.2. 1/4-Comma Meantone Temperament

Fifths				Major Thirds	
Interval	Tempering	Cents	Comma	Interval	Cents
C–G	–1/4 SC	696.5	–5.5	C–E	386
G–D	–1/4 SC	696.5	–5.5	G–B	386
D–A	–1/4 SC	696.5	–5.5	D–F♯	386
A–E	–1/4 SC	696.5	–5.5	A–C♯	386
E–B	–1/4 SC	696.5	–5.5	E–G♯	386
B–F♯	1/4 SC	696.5	–5.5	B–E♭	428
F♯–C♯	–1/4 SC	696.5	–5.5	F♯–B♭	428
C♯–G♯	–1/4 SC	696.5	–5.5	C♯–F	428
G♯–E♭	wolf	738.5	+36.5	G♯–C	428
E♭–B♭	–1/4 SC	696.5	–5.5	E♭–G	386
B♭–F	–1/4 SC	696.5	–5.5	B♭–D	386
F–C	–1/4 SC	696.5	–5.5	F–A	386

pure major third is formed by making each of its four constituent fifths narrower than pure by one-quarter of the syntonic comma (–1/4 SC). For example, the major third C–E is derived from the fifths C–G, G–D, D–A, and A–E. When each of those fifths is tempered –1/4 SC, then C–E is pure. This is the meaning of the term "1/4-comma," which refers to the syntonic, not Pythagorean, comma.

Narrowing fifths by one-quarter of the syntonic comma may be continued for eleven of the twelve fifths in the circle, resulting in eight pure major thirds. After tempering eleven of the fifths, the price is paid for all the pure thirds. Eleven fifths narrowed by 5.5 cents adds up to –60.5 cents (–5.5 × 11 = –60.5), which is far too much. To make the fourth column add up to –24 cents, the twelfth interval in the circle of fifths must be +36.5 cents. Such an interval is excessively wide and of limited musical usefulness; it is the G♯–E♭ interval in the list of fifths, and its size is 738.5 cents. It is known as the "wolf" interval because of the howling sound it makes, probably more so on the organ than the harpsichord. (While it is often referred to as a wolf "fifth," it is actually a diminished sixth.) The wolf interval may be considered a characteristic of meantone temperament; however, it should not be considered a musical attribute but rather a defect.[4] It is not an interval that is tempered; it is an interval that is left over after other intervals are tuned and tempered. Because of the wolf interval, four of the major thirds end up being very wide (428 cents) and also of limited musical usefulness. They are so wide that they are more like diminished fourths. The wolf interval and the four wide "thirds" are the intervals that are sacrificed in meantone temperament.

In other variations of meantone temperament, the fifths may be narrowed by 1/3, 2/7, 2/9, 1/5, 1/6, or 1/7 of the syntonic comma.[5] The 1/4-comma plan is quite popular because it results in so many pure major thirds and is easier to set than the others. For comparison, 1/6-comma meantone will be presented in detail later. Variants with fifths tempered less than one-quarter comma (2/9, 1/5, 1/6, 1/7) have major thirds that are wider than pure and smaller wolf intervals. Variants with fifths tempered more than one-quarter comma (1/3, 2/7) have major thirds that are narrower than pure and larger wolf intervals. The 1/3-comma plan has pure *minor* thirds. Any meantone temperament may be referred to as a regular temperament because any given variation has only one size fifth, excluding the wolf interval.

The term "meantone" is derived from the fact that for any pure major third, the note in the middle of the interval is exactly between the two outer notes. For example, with the major third C–E, D is tuned so that the interval C–D is the same size as the interval D–E, which is 193 cents, exactly half the amount of the pure major third, 386 cents. D is the average or "mean" tone between C and E.[6] (See chapter 3.)

Pythagorean tuning and meantone temperament are actually extreme plans. The former favors pure fifths at the expense of major thirds, while the latter favors pure major thirds at the expense of the fifths. Ironically, each scheme has defects or sacrifices in the very class of intervals it seeks to promote. Pythagorean tuning has a very narrow "fifth" amid eleven pure fifths, and meantone temperament has four very wide "thirds" among eight pure major thirds.

At the opposite end of the spectrum from Pythagorean tuning and meantone temperament is equal temperament (table 2.3). Although equal temperament is the youngest in terms of widespread use— becoming commonplace in the nineteenth century—it was used for fretted instruments such as the lute and viol in the early sixteenth century.[7] In equal temperament, the Pythagorean comma is divided equally among all twelve intervals in the circle of fifths, so every fifth is tempered narrower than pure by one-twelfth of the Pythagorean comma

Table 2.3. Equal Temperament

	Fifths			Major Thirds	
Interval	Tempering	Cents	Comma	Interval	Cents
C–G	–1/12 PC	700	–2	C–E	400
G–D	–1/12 PC	700	–2	G–B	400
D–A	–1/12 PC	700	–2	D–F♯	400
A–E	–1/12 PC	700	–2	A–C♯	400
E–B	–1/12 PC	700	–2	E–G♯	400
B–F♯	–1/12 PC	700	–2	B–E♭	400
F♯–C♯	–1/12 PC	700	–2	F♯–B♭	400
C♯–G♯	–1/12 PC	700	–2	C♯–F	400
G♯–E♭	–1/12 PC	700	–2	G♯–C	400
E♭–B♭	–1/12 PC	700	–2	E♭–G	400
B♭–F	–1/12 PC	700	–2	B♭–D	400
F–C	–1/12 PC	700	–2	F–A	400

(–1/12 PC) or two cents. (Some authors prefer to specify this two-cent tempering as one-eleventh of the syntonic comma or –1/11 SC.) Thus, all the fifths are 700 cents. Because all the fifths are the same size, the calculation of any major third produces the same answer: all major thirds are 400 cents. This is a simple and mathematically elegant solution for dealing with the Pythagorean comma.

Some people characterize equal temperament as a meantone temperament because it has "mean" tones and "regular" fifths. However, a true meantone temperament has a wolf interval. Equal temperament should be considered in a class by itself.

The middle ground between the extreme plans such as Pythagorean tuning and meantone temperament on the one hand and the simplistic compromise of equal temperament on the other is the class of *well-tempered systems*. A well-tempered system may be defined as a temperament in which there are (1) no unusable intervals such as a wolf or very wide "thirds" and (2) a combination of fifths of different sizes (and, as a consequence, thirds of different sizes). This last point—fifths of different sizes—accounts for the use of two terms: "irregular temperament," which is in contrast to meantone temperament with one size fifth (excluding the wolf), and "unequal temperament," which is in contrast to equal temperament. There is also the term "circulating temperament" which means one can play in or modulate through all the key signatures since there are no unusable intervals. The only term that is objectionable and should not be used is "well temperament."

Some people characterize equal temperament as a well-tempered system because there is no wolf interval, but, again, equal temperament should be its own category.

The group of well-tempered systems is by far the largest, and some of them are more mathematics than music. Many seventeenth- and eighteenth-century theorists compiled innumerable temperaments that were speculative and not intended for practical use.[8] This discussion will present several of the more notable and useful ones. As reference points for the major thirds, keep in mind the three main types already discussed: the pure major third of 386 cents, the equal temperament major third of 400 cents, and the Pythagorean major third of 408 cents.

Werckmeister III (table 2.4) is named after Andreas Werckmeister (1645–1706). This temperament was published in 1681 and again in 1691.[9] It may be the first documented temperament for keyboard instruments that did not have a wolf interval. It consists of four fifths tempered narrower than pure by one-quarter of the Pythagorean comma (–1/4 PC); these are C–G, G–D, D–A, and B–F♯. The other eight fifths are tuned pure. There are four different sizes of major thirds: 390, 396, 402, and 408 cents. Werckmeister III was originally meant for organs, but since it is often discussed and is easy to set, it is included here. It is supposedly the temperament that Werckmeister himself favored, and it was singled out by other theorists.[10]

Supposedly the above version is a theoretical model. Werckmeister himself suggested that in practice the fifths C–G, G–D, and D–A could be tempered by one-quarter of the *syntonic* comma (–1/4 SC, –5.5 cents) as in 1/4-comma meantone temperament.[11] Then, the fifth B–F♯ would be tempered one-quarter of the syntonic comma plus the schisma, or –7.5 cents. This is significant because an organ with an existing meantone temperament could be re-tuned to Werckmeister III relatively quickly, since not all of the pipes would need adjusting.[12]

Kirnberger III (table 2.5) is named for Johann Philipp Kirnberger (1721–1783), whose writings were published in the 1770s.[13] It consists of four fifths tempered narrower than pure by one-quarter of the syntonic comma (–1/4 SC): C–G, G–D, D–A, and A–E. In addition, there is one fifth narrower than pure by the schisma (–2 cents) which may be

Table 2.4. Werckmeister III

Fifths				Major Thirds	
Interval	Tempering	Cents	Comma	Interval	Cents
C–G	–1/4 PC	696	–6	C–E	390
G–D	–1/4 PC	696	–6	G–B	396
D–A	–1/4 PC	696	–6	D–F♯	396
A–E	pure	702	0	A–C♯	402
E–B	pure	702	0	E–G♯	402
B–F♯	–1/4 PC	696	–6	B–E♭	402
F♯–C♯	pure	702	0	F♯–B♭	408
C♯–G♯	pure	702	0	C♯–F	408
G♯–E♭	pure	702	0	G♯–C	408
E♭–B♭	pure	702	0	E♭–G	402
B♭–F	pure	702	0	B♭–D	396
F–C	pure	702	0	F–A	390

Table 2.5. Kirnberger III

Fifths				Major Thirds	
Interval	Tempering	Cents	Comma	Interval	Cents
C–G	–1/4 SC	696.5	–5.5	C–E	386
G–D	–1/4 SC	696.5	–5.5	G–B	391.5
D–A	–1/4 SC	696.5	–5.5	D–F♯	397
A–E	–1/4 SC	696.5	–5.5	A–C♯	402.5
E–B	pure	702	0	E–G♯	406
B–F♯	pure	702	0	B–E♭	406
F♯–C♯	–1/12 PC	700	–2	F♯–B♭	406
C♯–G♯	pure	702	0	C♯–F	408
G♯–E♭	pure	702	0	G♯–C	408
E♭–B♭	pure	702	0	E♭–G	402.5
B♭–F	pure	702	0	B♭–D	397
F–C	pure	702	0	F–A	391.5

notated as one-twelfth of the Pythagorean comma (–1/12 PC). The other seven fifths are tuned pure. There are six different sizes of major thirds; C–E is a pure major third because the fifths in the sequence C–G–D–A–E are tempered similar to the fifths found in meantone temperament. Jorgensen refers to "Aron-Neidhardt" temperament, which is similar to Kirnberger III except the schisma is at E–B.[14]

Vallotti temperament (table 2.6) was described by Francesco Antonio Vallotti (1697–1780) in 1779.[15] Giuseppe Tartini (1692–1770) mentioned Vallotti and this temperament in 1754.[16] It consists of six fifths tempered narrower than pure by one-sixth of the Pythagorean comma (–1/6 PC), with the other fifths tuned pure. The major thirds range from 392 to 408 cents. The presence of six adjacent pure fifths means this temperament has three Pythagorean thirds. Compare this with the next temperament.

Table 2.6. Vallotti

Fifths				Major Thirds	
Interval	Tempering	Cents	Comma	Interval	Cents
C–G	–1/6 PC	698	–4	C–E	392
G–D	–1/6 PC	698	–4	G–B	392
D–A	–1/6 PC	698	–4	D–F♯	396
A–E	–1/6 PC	698	–4	A–C♯	400
E–B	–1/6 PC	698	–4	E–G♯	404
B–F♯	pure	702	0	B–E♭	408
F♯–C♯	pure	702	0	F♯–B♭	408
C♯–G♯	pure	702	0	C♯–F	408
G♯–E♭	pure	702	0	G♯–C	404
E♭–B♭	pure	702	0	E♭–G	400
B♭–F	pure	702	0	B♭–D	396
F–C	–1/6 PC	698	–4	F–A	392

Young's temperament no. 2 (table 2.7) was described by Thomas Young (1773–1829) in 1800.[17] This is very similar to Vallotti. Both Vallotti and Young no. 2 have six fifths tempered narrower than pure

Table 2.7. Young No. 2

Fifths				Major Thirds	
Interval	Tempering	Cents	Comma	Interval	Cents
C–G	–1/6 PC	698	–4	C–E	392
G–D	–1/6 PC	698	–4	G–B	392
D–A	–1/6 PC	698	–4	D–F♯	392
A–E	–1/6 PC	698	–4	A–C♯	396
E–B	–1/6 PC	698	–4	E–G♯	400
B–F♯	–1/6 PC	698	–4	B–E♭	404
F♯–C♯	pure	702	0	F♯–B♭	408
C♯–G♯	pure	702	0	C♯–F	408
G♯–E♭	pure	702	0	G♯–C	408
E♭–B♭	pure	702	0	E♭–G	404
B♭–F	pure	702	0	B♭–D	400
F–C	pure	702	0	F–A	396

by one-sixth of the Pythagorean comma, but the tempered fifths in Young no. 2 are on C, G, D, A, E, and B, as opposed to F, C, G, D, A, and E in Vallotti. The sizes of the major thirds in Young no. 2 are the same as Vallotti, but the cent values are shifted to different note names. Another temperament by Young is described later.

Neidhardt's circulating temperament no. 1 (table 2.8) was described by Johann Georg Neidhardt (c1685–1739) in 1724.[18] Compared to Werckmeister III and Kirnberger III, there are more fifths tempered, and each is tempered by a smaller fraction of the Pythagorean comma. A temperament such as this is often referred to as "subtle" because there are tempered fifths of more than one size, no heavily tempered fifths, and a narrow range of major third sizes: 392 to 404 cents. Because more fifths are tempered, there are no sequences of four consecutive pure fifths anywhere and therefore no Pythagorean thirds.

J. G. Neidhardt was highly regarded for his temperament plans: mathematically precise and well-tempered in the best sense of the word. There is some circumstantial evidence that he was the theorist J. S. Bach respected the most.[19] J. G. Neidhardt categorized the degree of subtlety in a temperament according to the size of the community,

Table 2.8. Neidhardt Circulating Temperament No. 1

Fifths				Major Thirds	
Interval	Tempering	Cents	Comma	Interval	Cents
C–G	–1/6 PC	698	–4	C–E	392
G–D	–1/6 PC	698	–4	G–B	394
D–A	–1/6 PC	698	–4	D–F♯	396
A–E	–1/6 PC	698	–4	A–C♯	400
E–B	–1/12 PC	700	–2	E–G♯	404
B–F♯	–1/12 PC	700	–2	B–E♭	404
F♯–C♯	pure	702	0	F♯–B♭	404
C♯–G♯	pure	702	0	C♯–F	404
G♯–E♭	–1/12 PC	700	–2	G♯–C	404
E♭–B♭	–1/12 PC	700	–2	E♭–G	402
B♭–F	pure	702	0	B♭–D	400
F–C	pure	698	0	F–A	396

presumably based on the assumption that larger towns and cities had more musical sophistication, used more sharps and flats, and therefore needed a more refined temperament.

Tempérament ordinaire (table 2.9) is a general term for a "common" or "normal" temperament that was used in eighteenth-century France. Plans such as these are sometimes referred to as modified meantone temperaments. It has six fifths tempered narrower than pure by one-fifth of the Pythagorean comma (–1/5 PC), with the result that the major thirds on F, C, and G are 388 cents, very close to pure. Yet, it also has characteristics of a well-tempered system: no wolf interval, and fifths of various sizes. An interesting feature of this temperament is that there are two fifths tempered *wider* than pure (+1/10 PC). As a result, two of the major thirds are even larger than a Pythagorean third.

Since *tempérament ordinaire* is a "style" of tempering fifths rather than a specific mathematical plan, several different versions exist. The one given here is an approximation based on the information presented by Lindley.[20] In one variation, there are three pure fifths and three wide fifths; in another variation, there are seven narrow fifths instead of six. Another example by Rameau is given in table 2.11.

Table 2.9. *Tempérament Ordinaire*

Fifths				Major Thirds	
Interval	Tempering	Cents	Comma	Interval	Cents
C–G	–1/5 PC	697.2	–4.8	C–E	388.8
G–D	–1/5 PC	697.2	–4.8	G–B	388.8
D–A	–1/5 PC	697.2	–4.8	D–F♯	393.6
A–E	–1/5 PC	697.2	–4.8	A–C♯	398.4
E–B	–1/5 PC	697.2	–4.8	E–G♯	403.2
B–F♯	pure	702	0	B–E♭	408
F♯–C♯	pure	702	0	F♯–B♭	410.4
C♯–G♯	pure	702	0	C♯–F	412.8
G♯–E♭	pure	702	0	G♯–C	408
E♭–B♭	+1/10 PC	704.4	+2.4	E♭–G	403.2
B♭–F	+1/10 PC	704.4	+2.4	B♭–D	396
F–C	–1/5 PC	697.2	–4.8	F–A	388.8

The characteristic wider-than-pure fifths are apparently due to a misinterpretation of the tuning instructions given by Marin Mersenne in 1636 for a regular meantone temperament.[21] Mersenne gave instructions to tune b^b "forte" to f^1 and to tune e^b "forte" to b^b. Since he was dealing with meantone temperament, this should be taken to mean the note b^b is tuned sharp—raised in pitch—so the fifth b^b–f^1 is narrower than pure, and the note e^b is tuned sharp so the fifth e^b–b^b is also narrower than pure. The misinterpretation was to assume that the *intervals* should be tuned sharp; that is, wider than pure. Interestingly enough, this mistake turned out to be musically useful.

Similar in layout to 1/4-comma meantone temperament is 1/6-comma meantone temperament (table 2.10), but the fifths are tempered less in the latter. This means that the 1/6-comma variety has no pure major thirds, a smaller wolf interval, and the four wide "thirds" are not quite as wide. This plan is sometimes referred to as "Silbermann temperament" after the organbuilder Gottfried Silbermann. However, there is evidence that Silbermann's version was based on fifths tempered narrower than pure by one-sixth of the Pythagorean comma, or –4 cents.[22]

Table 2.10. 1/6-Comma Meantone Temperament

	Fifths			Major Thirds	
Interval	Tempering	Cents	Comma	Interval	Cents
C–G	–1/6 SC	698.3	–3.7	C–E	393.2
G–D	–1/6 SC	698.3	–3.7	G–B	393.2
D–A	–1/6 SC	698.3	–3.7	D–F♯	393.2
A–E	–1/6 SC	698.3	–3.7	A–C♯	393.2
E–B	–1/6 SC	698.3	–3.7	E–G♯	393.2
B–F♯	–1/6 SC	698.3	–3.7	B–E♭	413.6
F♯–C♯	–1/6 SC	698.3	–3.7	F♯–B♭	413.6
C♯–G♯	–1/6 SC	698.3	–3.7	C♯–F	413.6
G♯–E♭	wolf	718.7	+16.7	G♯–C	413.6
E♭–B♭	–1/6 SC	698.3	–3.7	E♭–G	393.2
B♭–F	–1/6 SC	698.3	–3.7	B♭–D	393.2
F–C	–1/6 SC	698.3	–3.7	F–A	393.2

Table 2.11 presents a modified meantone temperament described by Jean-Philippe Rameau (1683–1764) in 1726.[23] Notice seven fifths tempered narrower than pure by one-quarter of the syntonic comma, and two wide fifths characteristic of *tempérament ordinaire*.

Georg Andreas Sorge (1703–1778) was an eighteenth-century theorist who devised many subtle temperaments. The temperament given here (table 2.12) was published in 1744.[24]

Table 2.13 presents another temperament by Thomas Young from 1800;[25] compare this to Young no. 2, Neidhardt, and Sorge.

Herbert Kellner's temperament (table 2.14) is described as a reconstruction of J. S. Bach's tuning for *The Well-Tempered Clavier*.[26]

John Barnes' temperament (table 2.15) is based on a study of the intervals in J. S. Bach's *Well-Tempered Clavier*.[27]

Mark Lindley's temperament (table 2.16) is a modification of Werckmeister III with the organ music of J. S. Bach in mind.[28] The fact that it will be referred to here simply as "Lindley" does not imply that he devised only this plan.

Table 2.11. Rameau

	Fifths			Major Thirds	
Interval	Tempering	Cents	Comma	Interval	Cents
C–G	–1/4 SC	696.5	–5.5	C–E	386
G–D	–1/4 SC	696.5	–5.5	G–B	386
D–A	–1/4 SC	696.5	–5.5	D–F♯	391.5
A–E	–1/4 SC	696.5	–5.5	A–C♯	397
E–B	–1/4 SC	696.5	–5.5	E–G♯	402.5
B–F♯	pure	702	0	B–E♭	415.25
F♯–C♯	pure	702	0	F♯–B♭	422.5
C♯–G♯	pure	702	0	C♯–F	417
G♯–E♭	+1/3 SC	709.25	+7.25	G♯–C	411.5
E♭–B♭	+1/3 SC	709.25	+7.25	E♭–G	398.75
B♭–F	–1/4 SC	696.5	–5.5	B♭–D	386
F–C	–1/4 SC	696.5	–5.5	F–A	386

Table 2.12. Sorge

	Fifths			Major Thirds	
Interval	Tempering	Cents	Comma	Interval	Cents
C–G	–1/6 PC	698	–4	C–E	396
G–D	–1/6 PC	698	–4	G–B	396
D–A	–1/6 PC	698	–4	D–F♯	398
A–E	pure	702	0	A–C♯	400
E–B	–1/6 PC	698	–4	E–G♯	400
B–F♯	–1/12 PC	700	–2	B–E♭	404
F♯–C♯	–1/12 PC	700	–2	F♯–B♭	404
C♯–G♯	pure	702	0	C♯–F	404
G♯–E♭	pure	702	0	G♯–C	404
E♭–B♭	–1/12 PC	700	–2	E♭–G	400
B♭–F	–1/12 PC	700	–2	B♭–D	398
F–C	pure	702	0	F–A	396

Table 2.13. Young No. 1

	Fifths			Major Thirds	
Interval	Tempering	Cents	Comma	Interval	Cents
C–G	–1/6 PC	698	–4	C–E	392
G–D	–1/6 PC	698	–4	G–B	394
D–A	–1/6 PC	698	–4	D–F♯	396
A–E	–1/6 PC	698	–4	A–C♯	400
E–B	–1/12 PC	700	–2	E–G♯	404
B–F♯	–1/12 PC	700	–2	B–E♭	406
F♯–C♯	pure	702	0	F♯–B♭	408
C♯–G♯	pure	702	0	C♯–F	406
G♯–E♭	pure	702	0	G♯–C	404
E♭–B♭	pure	702	0	E♭–G	400
B♭–F	–1/12 PC	700	–2	B♭–D	396
F–C	–1/12 PC	700	–2	F–A	394

Table 2.14. Kellner

	Fifths			Major Thirds	
Interval	Tempering	Cents	Comma	Interval	Cents
C–G	–1/5 PC	697.2	–4.8	C–E	388.8
G–D	–1/5 PC	697.2	–4.8	G–B	393.6
D–A	–1/5 PC	697.2	–4.8	D–F♯	393.6
A–E	–1/5 PC	697.2	–4.8	A–C♯	398.4
E–B	pure	702	0	E–G♯	403.2
B–F♯	–1/5 PC	697.2	–4.8	B–E♭	403.2
F♯–C♯	pure	702	0	F♯–B♭	408
C♯–G♯	pure	702	0	C♯–F	408
G♯–E♭	pure	702	0	G♯–C	408
E♭–B♭	pure	702	0	E♭–G	403.2
B♭–F	pure	702	0	B♭–D	398.4
F–C	pure	702	0	F–A	393.6

Table 2.15. Barnes

	Fifths				Major Thirds	
Interval	Tempering	Cents	Comma		Interval	Cents
C–G	–1/6 PC	698	–4		C–E	392
G–D	–1/6 PC	698	–4		G–B	396
D–A	–1/6 PC	698	–4		D–F♯	396
A–E	–1/6 PC	698	–4		A–C♯	400
E–B	pure	702	0		E–G♯	404
B–F♯	–1/6 PC	698	–4		B–E♭	404
F♯–C♯	pure	702	0		F♯–B♭	408
C♯–G♯	pure	702	0		C♯–F	408
G♯–E♭	pure	702	0		G♯–C	404
E♭–B♭	pure	702	0		E♭–G	400
B♭–F	pure	702	0		B♭–D	396
F–C	–1/6 PC	698	–4		F–A	392

Table 2.16. Lindley

	Fifths				Major Thirds	
Interval	Tempering	Cents	Comma		Interval	Cents
C–G	–1/6 PC	698	–4		C–E	392
G–D	–1/6 PC	698	–4		G–B	392
D–A	–1/6 PC	698	–4		D–F♯	394
A–E	–1/6 PC	698	–4		A–C♯	398
E–B	–1/6 PC	698	–4		E–G♯	402
B–F♯	–1/12 PC	700	–2		B–E♭	406
F♯–C♯	pure	702	0		F♯–B♭	408
C♯–G♯	pure	702	0		C♯–F	408
G♯–E♭	pure	702	0		G♯–C	406
E♭–B♭	pure	702	0		E♭–G	402
B♭–F	pure	702	0		B♭–D	398
F–C	–1/12 PC	700	–2		F–A	394

The Just Scale

Mention should be made of the *just scale* as it contrasts with the concept of temperament discussed in chapter 1 and the specific temperaments discussed in this chapter. (As mentioned previously, in this context "just" is a synonym for "pure.") A just scale—commonly referred to as just intonation—is a theory of tuning based on pure octaves, pure fifths, and pure major thirds; more specifically, it is a scale in which the frequency relationships of the notes are according to small whole numbers, such as 2:1, 3:2, and 5:4. (Some people refer to the "natural-ness" of the just scale because it is based on the whole-number multipliers found in the harmonic series.) That is, any note in a just scale must have a pure relationship with one or more notes in the same scale. The appeal of the just scale is that pure intervals with simple frequency ratios are more pleasing, particularly when pure intervals are assembled into triads such as C–E–G and F–A–C. The problem is that it is not a practical tuning for keyboard instruments with twelve keys per octave. As discussed in chapter 1, pure octaves and pure fifths cannot co-exist on keyboard instruments, and pure fifths form major thirds that are wider than pure. One can generate a just scale up to a point, but the tuning discrepancies—the Pythagorean and syntonic commas—prevent one from creating a complete usable scale for keyboard instruments.[29] A just scale is an ideal for the sake of pure intervals, temperament is a compromise for the sake of practicality.[30]

One historical approach at dovetailing the concept of a just scale with the keyboard was through the use of *split sharps* or *subsemitones*.[31] This involved the use of sharp keys that were divided into a front and back half, with the back half raised slightly. Each half-key operated independently; so, in the example of a harpsichord, each had its own key lever, jack(s), and string(s). Each of the corresponding notes could then be tuned independently of the other. A split sharp between the D and E keys on the keyboard offered the performer both a D♯ and an E♭; a split sharp between the G and A keys offered both G♯ and A♭. With this approach, D♯ could be tuned as a pure major third with B, and E♭ could be tuned as a pure major third with G. Obviously this would have its advantages under some circumstances in terms of intonation. However, the complexities of fingering and hand position dictated by such a keyboard configuration presented problems. Split sharps offer alternate intonational possibilities, but, again, temperament offers practicality.

Sources of Confusion

Pythagorean vs. Syntonic Commas

There are instances in the literature in which the Pythagorean and syntonic commas are not differentiated. Even though the difference is small—2 cents—the mathematical representation of the fifths in a temperament should distinguish between them.

The shorthand version of the tempering in column two of the tables sometimes is in terms of the Pythagorean comma and sometimes is in terms of the syntonic comma. While there is a direct relationship with some temperaments and a specific tuning discrepancy—for example, 1/4-comma meantone temperament and the syntonic comma—the easiest rule to follow is: use the simpler ratio. For example, with a fifth tempered 6 cents, 6 is 25 percent of the Pythagorean comma but is 27.3 percent of the syntonic comma. In this case, the simpler ratio is −1/4 PC rather than −3/11 SC. Similarly, with a fifth tempered 5.5 cents, 5.5 is 25 percent of the syntonic comma but is 22.9 percent of the Pythagorean comma, so the simpler ratio is −1/4 SC rather than −11/48 PC. The characterization of a fifth tempered 2 cents as either −1/12 PC or −1/11 SC is a matter of personal preference.

Terminology

Some writers reserve the term "meantone" to refer only to 1/4-comma meantone temperament. Others use the term in a broader sense to refer to all the variants that have regular fifths and a wolf interval. The 1/4-comma plan is often given preferred status because it has so many pure major thirds.

Andreas Werckmeister referred to the temperament described above as "First Correct Temperament" in 1681 and as "Number III" in 1691. As a result, one may find references to it as "Werckmeister," Werckmeister I," and "Werckmeister III" (which is the one used most). Some refer to it as "Werckmeister's organ temperament."

Some references to Kirnberger temperament are disparaging. What this refers to is Kirnberger II, which has the fifths D–A and A–E both tempered −1/2 SC or −11 cents and F♯–C♯ tempered −2 cents. Such heavy tempering is far from subtle.

Many writers believe Vallotti and Young to be the same temperament; one will sometimes see mention of "Vallotti/Young" temperament. While they both have six adjacent fifths tempered by one-sixth of
the Pythagorean comma, the layout of those fifths is different between
the two temperaments. Sometimes Young no. 2 is referred to as "transposed Vallotti." Vallotti was re-discovered in 1970 by Jan van Biezen,
and so there are references to a "van Biezen" temperament.

Even though the words "Neidhardt" and "Sorge" are used to denote the temperaments described here, there are many plans by each
person. It is even more confusing because, for example, J. G. Neidhardt
himself categorized the same temperament in different ways at different
times. The unequivocal way to differentiate a temperament is by its
tempering pattern. One possible notation (after John Barnes) is

Neidhardt   4 4 4 4   2 2 0 0   2 2 0 0.

This gives the same information as was given in column 4 of tables 2.1
through 2.16 about the distribution of the Pythagorean comma, except
the negative signs are left out. The numbers are separated into three
groups of four based on the fifths C–G–D–A, E–B–F♯–C♯, and
G♯–E♭–B♭–F. Once the fifth tempering for each plan is understood,
the comma-based notation might prove useful as a means of avoiding
confusion when writing about temperament. This approach is most useful for differentiating the more subtle temperaments, such as Vallotti,
both Youngs, Neidhardt, Sorge, Barnes, and Lindley, that have fifths
tempered by both one-sixth and one-twelfth of the Pythagorean comma
(–4 and –2 cents respectively). These are summarized in table 2.17.

Table 2.17. Comma-Based Notation for Selected Temperaments

Name	Notation		
Vallotti	4 4 4 4	4 0 0 0	0 0 0 4
Young no. 2	4 4 4 4	4 4 0 0	0 0 0 0
Neidhardt	4 4 4 4	2 2 0 0	2 2 0 0
Sorge	4 4 4 0	4 2 2 0	0 2 2 0
Young no. 1	4 4 4 4	2 2 0 0	0 0 2 2
Barnes	4 4 4 4	0 4 0 0	0 0 0 4
Lindley	4 4 4 4	4 2 0 0	0 0 0 2

It should be mentioned that some temperaments are characterized by a similar group of numbers that represent the cent deviations from equal temperament. This is *not* what the above notation represents. Cent deviations will be discussed in chapter 13.

Classification

Table 2.18 lists four main categories of temperament—meantone, modified meantone, the well-tempered systems, and equal temperament—classified according to the following descriptions:

regular: fifths of only one size, with or without a wolf interval
irregular: fifths of various sizes
equal: all fifths the same size, no pure fifths
unequal: fifths of various sizes
circulating: allows modulation through all key signatures
    (all fifths and major thirds are usable)
non-circulating: does not allow modulation though all key signatures (at least one fifth or one major third is unusable)

Table 2.18. Classification of Temperaments

Meantone Temperaments[a]	Modified Meantone Temperaments[b]	Well-Tempered Systems[c]	Equal Temperament[d]
regular, with wolf	irregular	irregular	regular, no wolf
non-circulating	non-circulating	circulating	circulating
———	unequal	unequal	equal

a. Includes all varieties: 1/4-comma, 1/5-comma, 1/6-comma, and so on
b. Includes *tempérament ordinaire* and Rameau
c. Includes Werkmeister III, Kirnberger III, Vallotti, both Youngs, Neidhardt, Sorge, Kellner, Barnes, and Lindley
d. Includes only equal temperament

The terms "irregular" and "unequal" are synonymous—meaning fifths of various sizes—but their points of reference differ: "irregular" is in contrast to a regular temperament such as one of the meantone temperaments or equal temperament, while "unequal" is in contrast to only equal temperament. An irregular or unequal temperament may or may not have one or more pure fifths. The term "circulating" is usually not defined in terms of fifths or thirds. However, for our purpose, reference to fifths and thirds is useful because the modified meantone temperaments—*tempérament ordinaire* and Rameau—have usable fifths but very wide major thirds that probably should be considered musically limited. Thus, these temperaments are listed as "non-circulating."

Summary

Pythagorean tuning features eleven pure fifths. The twelfth interval in the circle of fifths is an interval that is narrower than pure by the whole Pythagorean comma and is of limited use. The wide major thirds of 408 cents are called Pythagorean thirds.

A characteristic of 1/4-comma meantone temperament is eight pure major thirds (386 cents). These are formed by having eleven fifths in the circle of fifths tempered by one-quarter of the syntonic comma. The twelfth interval is an extremely wide diminished sixth that is called the "wolf" interval. It is of limited use and causes four of the major thirds to be of limited use.

Equal temperament has the Pythagorean comma divided evenly among all twelve intervals in the circle of fifths, so all fifths are the same size (700 cents), and all major thirds are the same size (400 cents).

Well-tempered systems are those in which there are no unusable intervals such as the heavily-tempered "fifth" in Pythagorean tuning or the wolf in meantone temperament, and there are fifths of different sizes, which is the reason these are sometimes referred to as unequal or irregular temperaments. Because the fifths are of different sizes, the thirds are also of different sizes, which offer tonal variety among the key signatures.

Representative temperaments include Werckmeister III, Kirnberger III, Vallotti, Young no. 2, Neidhardt circulating temperament no. 1, 1/6-comma meantone temperament, *tempérament ordinaire*, Rameau, Sorge, Young no. 1, Kellner, Barnes, and Lindley.

Sources for Temperaments

Print

Barbour, J. Murray. *Tuning and Temperament: A Historical Survey.* East Lansing: Michigan State College Press, 1951. Reprint New York: DaCapo Press, 1972. Reprint Mineola, N.Y.: Dover Publications, 2004.

Di Veroli, Claudio. *Unequal Temperaments and Their Role in the Performance of Early Music.* Buenos Aires: Artes Gráficas Farro, 1978.

Jorgensen, Owen. *Tuning: Containing the Perfection of Eighteenth-Century Temperament, the Lost Art of Nineteenth-Century Temperament, and the Science of Equal Temperament, Complete with Instructions for Aural and Electronic Tuning.* East Lansing: Michigan State University Press, 1991.

―――. *Tuning the Historical Temperaments by Ear.* Marquette: Northern Michigan University Press, 1977.

Klop, G. C. *Harpsichord Tuning.* Translated by Glen Wilson. Garderen, Holland: Werkplaats voor Clavecimbelbouw, 1974. Reprint, 1983.

Lindley, Mark. "Tuning and Intonation." 169–85 in *Performance Practice: Music after 1600.* The Norton/Grove Handbooks in Music, edited by Howard Mayer Brown and Stanley Sadie. New York: W. W. Norton & Company, 1989.

―――. "Well-Tempered Clavier." 3:847–49 in *The New Grove Dictionary of Musical Instruments,* 3 vols., edited by Stanley Sadie. London: Macmillan Press, 1984.

McNeil, Michael. "An Analysis Tool for Contemporary and Historical Tunings." *Diapason* 78 (February 1978): 14–16.

Rensch, Richard. "The Kirnberger Temperament and Its Effect on Organ Sound." *ISO Information* 12 (April 1974): 831–40.

Tittle, Martin B. *A Performer's Guide through Historical Keyboard Tunings.* Rev. ed. Ann Arbor, Mich.: Anderson Press, 1987.

Vogel, Harald. "Tuning and Temperament in the North German School of the Seventeenth and Eighteenth Centuries." 237–65 in *Charles Brenton Fisk, Organ Builder, Vol. I: Essays in His Honor,* edited by Fenner Douglass, Owen Jander, and Barbara Owen. Easthampton, Mass.: Westfield Center, 1986.

Wolf, Albrecht. "Graphic Representation and Functional Systematics of Historic Musical Temperaments." *ISO Information* 21 (December 1980): 41–70.

Internet

Beebe, Carey. "Resources: Technical Library: Tuning, Temperament." 2003. http:// www.hpschd.nu (12 July 2003).

Broekaert, Johan. "Harmony and Melody: The Tuning of Classic Music Instrumentation by Means of Objective Pitch Measurement." 2002. http:// home.tiscali.be/johan.broekaert3/Tuning_English.html (30 August 2003).

Claviers Baroques. "Schedule for Tuning Various Temperaments Using an Electronic Tuner with Meter." 2004. http://www.claviersbaroques.com/ CBExpertTemperamentsWithMeter.htm (22 November 2004).

Di Veroli, Claudio. "Unequal Temperaments." 2003. http://temper.braybaroque .ie (16 September 2003).

Duffin, Ross. "Tuning System Spreadsheets." 2003. http://music.cwru.edu/ duffin/tuning/Rec/default.html (9 September 2003).

Grönewald, Jürgen. "128 Musikalische Temperaturen im Mikrotonalen Vergleich." n.d. http://www.groenewald-berlin.de/Inhaltsverzeichnis.htm (3 January 2005).

Kanter, Jason. "About Temperaments." 2003. http://www.rollingball.com/ TemperamentsFrames.html (1 September 2003).

Kellner, Herbert A. "Instructions for Tuning a Harpsichord 'Wohltemperirt.'" n.d. http://ha.kellner.bei.t-online.de (9 September 2003).

Lehman, Bradley. "Keyboard Temperament Analyzer/Calculator." 2000. http:// www-personal.umich.edu/~bpl/temper.html *or* http://how.to/tune (18 July 2003).

Lewis, Pierre. "Understanding Temperaments." 1998. http://pages.globetrotter .net/roule/temper.htm (30 June 2003).

Poletti, Paul. "Temperaments for Dummies." 2001/2003. http://www .polettipiano.com/Media/T4D.PDF (9 September 2003).

Taylor, Nigel. "Tuning, Temperament, and Bells." n.d. http://www.kirnberger .fsnet.co.uk (24 August 2003).

Notes

1. Mark Lindley, "Instructions for the Clavier Diversely Tempered," *Early Music* 5 (January 1977): 19.

2. Margo Schulter, "Pythagorean Tuning and Medieval Polyphony," 1998, http://www.medieval.org/emfaq/harmony/pyth.html (27 June 2003).

3. Bartolomeo Ramos de Pareja, *Musica practica* (Bologna, 1482); and Pietro Aaron, *Thoscanello de la musica* (Venice, 1523).

4. William Porter, "The Meaning of Mean-Tone Temperament," *The American Organist* 15 (December 1981): 36.

5. Owen Jorgensen, *Tuning the Historical Temperaments by Ear* (Marquette: Northern Michigan University Press, 1977), 423; and Mark Lindley, "Temperaments," in *The New Grove Dictionary of Musical Instruments*, 3 vols., ed. Stanley Sadie (London: Macmillan Press, 1984), 3:541.

6. John Backus, *The Acoustical Foundations of Music*, 2nd ed. (New York: W. W. Norton & Company, 1977), 142; and Claudio Di Veroli, *Unequal Temperaments and Their Role in the Performance of Early Music* (Buenos Aires: Artes Gráficas Farro, 1978), 51.

7. Lindley, "Temperaments," *New Grove*, 551.

8. Lindley, "Temperaments," *New Grove*, 549.

9. Andreas Werckmeister, *Orgel-Probe* (Frankfurt/Main, 1681); Andreas Werckmeister, *Musicalische Temperatur* (Quedlinburg, 1691); and Kerala J. Snyder, "Bach and Buxtehude at the Large Organ of St. Mary's in Lübeck," in *Charles Brenton Fisk, Organ Builder, Vol. I: Essays in His Honor*, ed. Fenner Douglass, Owen Jander, and Barbara Owen (Easthampton, Mass.: Westfield Center, 1986), 186.

10. Mark Lindley, "Well-Tempered Clavier," in *The New Grove Dictionary of Musical Instruments*, 3 vols., ed. Stanley Sadie (London: Macmillan Press, 1984), 3:847; and Snyder, "Bach and Buxtehude," 186.

11. Lindley, "Well-Tempered Clavier," 847.

12. Lindley, "Temperaments," *New Grove*, 545, 549.

13. Johann Philipp Kirnberger, *Die Kunst des reinen Satzes in der Musik, II* (Königsberg, 1776–1779).

14. Owen Jorgensen, *The Equal-Beating Temperaments*, 2nd ed. (Hendersonville, N.C.: Sunbury Press, 2000), 26; and Jorgensen, *Tuning the Historical Temperaments*, 309–16.

15. Francesco Antonio Vallotti, *Della scienza teorica e pratica della moderna musica* (Padua, 1779).

16. Giuseppe Tartini, *Trattato di musica secondo la vera scienza dell' armonia* (Padua, 1754).

17. Thomas Young, "Outlines of Experiments and Inquiries Respecting Sound and Light," *Philosophical Transactions of the Royal Society of London* 90 (London, 1800): 145.

18. J. Murray Barbour, *Tuning and Temperament: A Historical Survey* (East Lansing: Michigan State College Press, 1951. Reprint, New York: DaCapo Press, 1972. Reprint, Mineola, N.Y.: Dover Publications, 2004), 167; and William Blood, "'Well-Tempering' the Clavier: Five Methods," *Early Music* 7 (October 1979): 495.

19. Mark Lindley, "Tuning and Intonation," in *Performance Practice: Music after 1600*. The Norton/Grove Handbooks in Music, ed. Howard Mayer Brown and Stanley Sadie (New York: W. W. Norton & Company, 1989), 180.

20. Lindley, "Well-Tempered Clavier," 848.

21. Lindley, "Temperaments," *New Grove*, 543; and Lindley, "Tuning and Intonation," 177, 179.

22. Helmut K. H. Lange, "Gottfried Silbermann's Organ Tuning: A Contribution to the Manner of Performing Ancient Music, Part II," *ISO Information* 9 (February 1973): 650–52; and Peter Williams, *The Organ Music of J. S. Bach, Vol. III: A Background* (Cambridge: Cambridge University Press, 1984), 188.

23. Jean-Philippe Rameau, *Nouveau système de musique théorique* (Paris, 1726).

24. Georg Andreas Sorge, *Anweisung zur Stimmung und Temperatur in einem Gespräch* (Hamburg, 1744); and Lindley, "Well-Tempered Clavier," 849.

25. Young, "Outlines of Experiments," 145; and Lindley, "Well-Tempered Clavier," 49.

26. Herbert A. Kellner, *The Tuning of My Harpsichord* (Frankfurt/Main: Verlag Das Musikinstrument, 1980), 40–45.

27. John Barnes, "Bach's Keyboard Temperament: Internal Evidence from the *Well-Tempered Clavier*," *Early Music* 7 (April 1979): 236–49.

28. Lindley, "Tuning and Intonation," 182–83.

29. Backus, *Acoustical Foundations*, 143–46.

30. Bruce Haynes, *A History of Performing Pitch: The Story of "A"* (Lanham, Md.: Scarecrow Press, 2002), 190.

31. Thomas Donahue, *The Modern Classical Organ: A Guide to Its Physical and Musical Structure and Performance Implications* (Jefferson, N.C.: McFarland & Company, 1991), 135–39.

3

Musical Aspects

While a temperament may be described in terms of the sizes of its fifths, its musical value is better revealed by a study of its major thirds, semitones, and key signatures. The following discussion will present an overview of these aspects for 1/4-comma meantone temperament, Werckmeister III, and equal temperament. This will give the performer one way of understanding the relationship of a particular temperament to the elements of music.

The note names C, C♯, D, E♭, and so on, will be used to identify not only notes but also key signatures and triads. To avoid confusion, each use will be specifically identified. We will also use the convention of denoting major keys and triads with uppercase letters and minor keys and triads with lowercase letters.

1/4-Comma Meantone Temperament

This temperament allows the performance of music in the key signatures B♭, F, C, G, D, A, g, d, and a. These have good tonic, subdominant, and dominant triads (that is, the I, IV, and V degrees of the scale). The major triad E and the minor triads e, b, f♯, and c♯ are usable, but they do not have good dominant triads (B, F♯, C♯, G♯). The major triad E♭ and the minor triad c are likewise usable, but they do not have good subdominant triads (A♭, f).

The semitones are two different sizes (table 3.1). (Notice that the distance between the notes C and D is 76 + 117 = 193 cents, and the distance between the notes D and E is 117 + 76 = 193 cents, so that D is the "mean" tone between C and E, which is 386 cents.) The wider intervals are called *diatonic semitones* and may be characterized by the fact that they are notated with two different note names. The narrower

Table 3.1. Semitone Size in 1/4-Comma Meantone Temperament

Semitone	Cents	Semitone	Cents
C–C♯	76	F♯–G	117
C♯–D	117	G–G♯	76
D–E♭	117	G♯–A	117
E♭–E	76	A–B♭	117
E–F	117	B♭–B	76
F–F♯	76	B–C	117

intervals are called *chromatic semitones*, with the same note name used, except a flat or sharp is added to one or the other.[1] Among the diatonic semitones, if one thinks of the lower note as the leading tone or seventh degree of the diatonic scale and the higher note as the tonic note, each diatonic semitone except D–E♭ coincides with a usable key signature. For example, with C♯–D, C♯ is the leading tone, D is the tonic note, and this corresponds to the usable key signatures of D and d. The exception to this—the key signature of E♭—can sometimes be used in an altered form of meantone temperament in which the note G♯ is retuned to be usable as an A♭. The practice of re-tuning certain notes to accommodate the music at hand, while seemingly useful in some respects, is only mentioned in one historical source.[2] The extent to which it was done is not known.

Among the usable key signatures, for every tonic chord with its pure major third there is also a dominant chord with a pure major third. Therefore, the movement from dominant to tonic involves the juxtaposition of very stable chords; meantone temperament is said to be suited for music with a strong harmonic or "vertical" character.[3] The leading tone—the seventh degree of the scale—is unmistakably associated with the dominant chord. (It should be noted that a low leading tone in relation to the tonic note is just another way of describing a wide diatonic semitone.) However, low leading tones are sometimes considered melodically poor; higher leading tones are said to be more expressive, since they seem to naturally want to resolve to the tonic.[4] This may be a reason for the use of ornamentation on the leading tones of the dominant triads, to anticipate the tonic in a way the note itself cannot. Variants of meantone temperament in which the fifths are tempered less—

1/5-comma or 1/6-comma—have slightly wider thirds and thus slightly higher leading tones compared to the 1/4-comma plan. These variants may provide more melodic interest in some musical situations.[5]

One particularly good melodic effect in 1/4-comma meantone temperament involves the alternation between diatonic and chromatic semitones in step-wise passages.[6] This is illustrated in table 3.2 with the note sequence A→G♯→G→F♯→F→E and the effect of alternating tension and relaxation. This effect is particularly effective if the lower note of a diatonic semitone (G♯, F♯, E) is the third in the triad of the prevailing harmony (E triad, D triad, C triad).

Table 3.2. Tension and Relaxation Effect of Meantone Semitones

Note Sequence	Semitone Type	Semitone Size (Cents)	Effect
A			
↓	diatonic	117	relaxation
G♯			
↓	chromatic	76	tension
G			
↓	diatonic	117	relaxation
F♯			
↓	chromatic	76	tension
F			
↓	diatonic	117	relaxation
E			

Another strong indicator of meantone temperament is the specific notation of the sharps and flats. Strict 1/4-comma meantone temperament provides the notes C♯, E♭, F♯, G♯, and B♭, not D♭, D♯, G♭, A♭, or A♯. For example, the note C♯ forms a pure third with A, not F, so it is not a D♭ and would not be notated in the music as a D♭. In some temperaments in which "C♯/D♭" forms a good third with either notes A or F, it would be notated as "C♯" when associated with an A and as "D♭" when associated with an F. Notes that are spelled differently but represent the same sound or pitch are called *enharmonic notes*. In meantone temperament, there are no enharmonic notes.

While there are obvious restrictions in meantone temperament related to the presence of "wrong enharmonics"—that is, the music calls for a D♯ but the temperament provides an E♭—there are several instances in which the "wrong note" may be acceptable—for example, as passing tones, in rapid passages, in augmented triads (C–E–G♯), and in diminished seventh chords (C–E♭–F♯–A).[7]

One also has to deal with the wolf interval. Generally it was avoided, but it may have been used for dramatic, tragic, comic, or other effects.[8] One can sometimes minimize the effect of a wolf interval by placing the wolf note off the beat (rhythmic displacement) or masking it by means of ornamentation.[9] Generally speaking, "harmonically sophisticated" music does not sound in tune played on a temperament with a wolf interval.[10]

Werckmeister III

In this temperament there is no wolf interval, so we do not need to discuss usable and unusable key signatures. However, it is important to note that the major and minor thirds are of different sizes (table 3.3), which produces slightly varied intonational characteristics among the different key signatures. It is notable that the triads with the purest major thirds also have the purest minor thirds; for example, B♭–D–F and F–A–C. Likewise, the triads with the least pure major thirds also have the least pure minor thirds. The musical significance of the variety of thirds is that movement or progression from more pure to less pure may be perceived as tension (for example, the chord progressions B♭→E♭ and C→f) and from less pure to more pure as relaxation (A→d, B→e, E→a). As a consequence, chord progressions such as A→D→B→e [11] and g→F→E♭→D [12] offer tonal variety and contribute interest in what would otherwise be static harmony.[13]

The tonic, subdominant, dominant, and relative minor triads (I, IV, V, and vi) in the key signatures of F, C, and G all have close-to-pure thirds. The key signature of F is quite exceptional, since there are not only close-to-pure thirds, but the fifths on F and B♭ are pure, making these very stable triads. The key signatures of F, C, and G would thus not exhibit as much interplay between tension and relaxation as other key signatures but would rather give a sense of stability and repose similar to meantone temperament.

This last point illustrates a typical pattern in many well-tempered systems: the fifths around C, G, D, and A are more tempered, so their

Table 3.3. Sizes of Thirds in Werckmeister III, in Cents

MAJOR THIRDS (pure = 386 cents)					
Most Pure		**Intermediate**		**Least Pure**	
B♭–D	396	E♭–G	402	F♯–B♭	408
F–A	390	A–C♯	402	C♯–F	408
C–E	390	E–G♯	402	G♯–C	408
G–B	396	B–E♭	402		
D–F♯	396				

MINOR THIRDS (pure = 316 cents)					
Most Pure		**Intermediate**		**Least Pure**	
d–f	306	g–b♭	300	e♭–f♯	294
a–c	312	b–d	300	b♭–c♯	294
e–g	306	f♯–a	300	f–g♯	294
		c♯–e	300	c–e♭	294
		g♯–b	300		

major thirds tend toward pure (386 cents), while the fifths around F♯, C♯, G♯, and E♭ are more pure, so their major thirds tend toward Pythagorean (408 cents). This makes the key signatures F, C, and G resemble meantone temperament and the key signatures F♯, C♯, and G♯ resemble Pythagorean tuning. This pattern is found in Werckmeister III, Kirnberger III, Vallotti, Young no. 2, Kellner, Barnes, and Lindley.

The semitones in Werckmeister III are given in table 3.4. While a sense of the diatonic and chromatic semitones still exists, the distinction is quite a bit less than in meantone temperament. This is a reflection of the wider major thirds and the higher leading tones.

Other well-tempered systems have general characteristics that are similar to Werckmeister III—various sizes of fifths and major thirds, no unusable key signatures, slight variations in semitone sizes—but they will differ in some details, such as the range of sizes of major thirds and the number of Pythagorean thirds. Werckmeister III was originally presented as a temperament for organs, and some believe it sounds more fitting for late seventeenth- and early eighteenth-century German organ

Table 3.4. Semitone Size in Werckmeister III

Semitone	Cents	Semitone	Cents
C–C♯	90	F♯–G	108
C♯–D	102	G–G♯	96
D–E♭	102	G♯–A	96
E♭–E	96	A–B♭	108
E–F	108	B♭–B	96
F–F♯	90	B–C	108

music.[14] The more subtle irregular temperaments (at least Vallotti, more typically Neidhardt) are usually most appropriate for late eighteenth-century music. There is evidence, however, that less subtle temperaments persisted in the eighteenth century in Italy, England, and France.[15]

Equal Temperament

With equal temperament, there is no need to discuss usable and unusable key signatures as in meantone temperament, because all are usable. There is also no need to discuss different sizes of thirds as in an unequal temperament, because all the thirds are the same size. Similarly, there is no distinction between wide and narrow semitones, because there is only one semitone size. So, a way we may characterize equal temperament is that it allows one to play in any key signature and to modulate from any one key signature to any other. Another way to describe it is based on the way it is sometimes set: all major thirds are equally sharp or wide so that each one beats no slower than the one below and no faster than the one above.[16] Because of how fast the major thirds in equal temperament beat—for example, 10 beats per second at c^1—they have been variously described as "nervous,"[17] "hectic,"[18] and "unresonant."[19]

The more enharmonic notes that are present in the music (both C♯ and D♭, both D♯ and E♭, both F♯ and G♭, etc.) and the more modulations there are to distant key signatures (B, F♯, D♭), the more the use of equal temperament is required.[20] If there is chromaticism that does not suggest any particular effect of alternating tension and relaxation, this points to the uniform semitones of equal temperament.[21]

Comparison of Major Thirds

Tables 3.5 and 3.6 provide information about the number, distribution, and range of different sizes of major thirds in the temperaments discussed in chapter 2. Table 3.5 summarizes those plans with only one or two sizes of major thirds: Pythagorean tuning, 1/4-comma meantone temperament, 1/6-comma meantone temperament, and equal temperament. Table 3.6 summarizes all the others. The reference values are the pure major third of 386 cents, the equal temperament major third of 400 cents, and the Pythagorean third of 408 cents. Generally speaking, the most harmonious major thirds range from 386 to 400 cents. Between 400 and 408 cents, the sound becomes more "coarse" or "nervous," with 408 cents being about the limit to the size of a usable major third. However, what is harmonious or not is open to question. Someone conditioned to modern pianos with equal temperament may have a high tolerance for major thirds of 400 cents, while someone used to hearing major thirds closer to pure might find 400-cent thirds harsh.

Table 3.5. Plans with One or Two Sizes of Major Thirds

Name	Sizes	Tonic Notes
Pythagorean tuning	384 cents	B, F♯, C♯, G♯
	408 cents	E♭, B♭, F, C, G, D, A, E
1/4-comma meantone	386 cents	E♭, B♭, F, C, G, D, A, E
	428 cents	B, F♯, C♯, G♯
1/6-comma meantone	393 cents	E♭, B♭, F, C, G, D, A, E
	414 cents	B, F♯, C♯, G♯
equal temperament	400 cents	all

Table 3.6. Cent Values of Major Thirds of Selected Temperaments

Cents	Werckmeister III	Kirnberger III	Vallotti
386		C	
387			
388			
389			
390	C, F		
391			
392		G, F	C, G, F
393			
394			
395			
396	G, D, B♭		D, B♭
397		D, B♭	
398			
399			
400			A, E♭
401			
402	A, E, B, E♭		
403		A, E♭	
404			E, G♯
405			
406		E, B, F♯	
407			
408	F♯, C♯, G♯	C♯, G♯	B, F♯, C♯
409			
410			
411			
412			
413			
414			
415			
416			
417			

(*continued on next page*)

Table 3.6 (*continued*)

Cents	Young 2	Neidhardt	Sorge
386			
387			
388			
389			
390			
391			
392	C, G, D	C	
393			
394		G	
395			
396	A, F	D, F	C, G, F
397			
398			D, B♭
399			
400	E, B♭	A, B♭	A, E, E♭
401			
402		E♭	
403			
404	B, E♭	E, B, F♯, C♯, G♯	B, F♯, C♯, G♯
405			
406			
407			
408	F♯, C♯, G♯		
409			
410			
411			
412			
413			
414			
415			
416			
417			

(*continued on next page*)

Table 3.6 (*continued*)

Cents	Rameau[a]	*Ordinaire*	Young 1
386	C, G, B♭, F		
387			
388			
389		C, G, F	
390			
391			
392	D		C
393			
394		D	G, F
395			
396		B♭	D, B♭
397	A		
398		A	
399	E♭		
400			A, E♭
401			
402			
403	E	E, E♭	
404			E, G♯
405			
406			B, C♯
407			
408		B, G♯	F♯
409			
410		F♯	
411			
412	G♯		
413		C♯	
414			
415	B		
416			
417	C♯		

a. In Rameau's temperament, the major third on F♯ is 423 cents.
(*continued on next page*)

Table 3.6 (*continued*)

Cents	Kellner	Barnes	Lindley
386			
387			
388			
389	C		
390			
391			
392		C, F	C, G
393			
394	G, D, F		D, F
395			
396		G, D, B♭	
397			
398	A, B♭		A, B♭
399			
400		A, E♭	
401			
402			E, E♭
403	E, B, E♭		
404		E, B, G♯	
405			
406			B, G♯
407			
408	F♯, C♯, G♯	F♯, C♯	F♯, C♯
409			
410			
411			
412			
413			
414			
415			
416			
417			

Summary

The performance of music in 1/4-comma meantone temperament is limited to key signatures with three or fewer sharps and two or fewer flats. The semitones are two sizes. The wider semitones tend to represent the leading tone and tonic note in the usable keys (the seventh and eighth degrees of the diatonic scale). The combination of a low leading tone and pure major thirds means that the movement from dominant to tonic triads (V to I) involves the juxtaposition of very stable chords. This suits music with a strong "vertical" harmonic character. The alternation of wide and narrow semitones also adds interest in chromatic passages. The sharps and flats in meantone are specifically C♯, E♭, F♯, G♯, and B♭, due to their association with the notes G, D, A, and E as pure major thirds. While some out-of-tune situations may be masked or subdued with rhythmic displacement of notes or with ornamentation, it should be recognized that some errant intervals may have been used for the specific purpose of producing an unusual effect.

Werckmeister III is a well-tempered system that has fifths of various sizes but no wolf interval. There are no unusable key signatures. The major and minor thirds throughout the different keys have a variety of sizes which offers harmonic interest, particularly with the chord progressions that were typical in the Baroque era. While there are semitones of different sizes, the distinction is less compared to the semitones in meantone temperament.

Equal temperament has equal-size fifths, equal-size thirds, and equal-size semitones. All keys are usable. Music with enharmonics, uniform semitone treatment, and equally-important key signatures all point to equal temperament.

Notes

1. Claudio Di Veroli, *Unequal Temperaments and Their Role in the Performance of Early Music* (Buenos Aires: Artes Gráficas Farro, 1978), 74.
2. Mark Lindley, "Temperaments," in *The New Grove Dictionary of Musical Instruments*, 3 vols., ed. Stanley Sadie (London: Macmillan Press, 1984), 3:546; and Rudolf Rasch, "Does 'Well-Tempered' Mean 'Equal-Tempered'?" in *Bach, Handel, Scarlatti: Tercentenary Essays*, ed. Peter Williams (Cambridge: Cambridge University Press, 1985), 307.

3. William Porter, "The Meaning of Mean-Tone Temperament," *The American Organist* 15 (December 1981): 36; and Richard Troeger, *Technique and Interpretation on the Harpsichord and Clavichord* (Bloomington: Indiana University Press, 1987), 211.

4. Mark Lindley, "An Historical Survey of Meantone Temperaments to 1620," *Early Keyboard Journal* 8 (1990): 12–13.

5. Lindley, "An Historical Survey," 12.

6. Porter, "The Meaning of Mean-Tone," 36.

7. Owen Jorgensen, *Tuning the Historical Temperaments by Ear* (Marquette: Northern Michigan University Press, 1977), 115–17.

8. Jorgensen, *Tuning the Historical Temperaments*, 115–17.

9. Jorgensen, *Tuning the Historical Temperaments*, 115–17.

10. Mark Lindley, "Tuning and Intonation," in *Performance Practice: Music after 1600*. The Norton/Grove Handbooks in Music, ed. Howard Mayer Brown and Stanley Sadie (New York: W. W. Norton & Company, 1989), 177.

11. Lindley, "Temperaments," *New Grove*, 547.

12. Lindley, "Temperaments," *New Grove*, 543–44.

13. Lindley, "Temperaments," *New Grove*, 547.

14. Lindley, "Temperaments," *New Grove*, 548.

15. Lindley, "Temperaments," *New Grove*, 548.

16. Lindley, "Temperaments," *New Grove*, 550.

17. Mark Lindley, "Some Thoughts Concerning the Effects of Tuning on Selected Musical Works (from Landini to Bach)," *Performance Practice Review* 9 (Spring 1996): 117.

18. David Ledbetter, *Bach's* Well-Tempered Clavier: *The 48 Preludes and Fugues* (New Haven: Yale University Press, 2002), 36.

19. Bruce Haynes, "Beyond Temperament: Non-Keyboard Intonation in the 17th and 18th Centuries," *Early Music* 19 (August 1991): 358.

20. Troeger, *Technique and Interpretation*, 216.

21. Troeger, *Technique and Interpretation*, 211.

4

Generating Tuning Instructions

This chapter demonstrates the calculations that take us from the mathematical representation of a temperament to the instructions for setting it on an instrument. For this purpose, we will use Werckmeister III.

Calculating Frequencies

First, we need to determine the frequencies of the notes in the tenor octave, c to b. This involves taking the cent values of the fifths, converting them to frequency ratios, and then using the frequency ratios to calculate frequencies from a reference pitch. Here we have our first encounter with the question of whether to use rounded or precise values for the calculations. The result we are looking for—beat rates for selected intervals—will vary by only a few tenths of a beat between the rounded and precise calculations, which is a negligible difference for all practical purposes. Even so, there is an advantage to using the precise values, which will be explained later. For purposes of comparison, table 4.1 lists both rounded and precise values. The derivations of the precise values are given at the end of the chapter.

We start with the precise cent values of the Werckmeister III fifths (table 4.2) and convert them to frequency ratios. This is done using a rearranged version of the cent equation, which is

$$\text{frequency ratio} = 10^{(\text{cent value} \div 3986.3137)}.$$

While this equation looks intimidating, it is easy to calculate on a scientific calculator with a 10^x key. Using the precise cent value of 696.090

59

Table 4.1. Rounded and Precise Temperament Values

Name	Rounded	Precise
cent equation constant	3986	3986.3137
pure fifth, in cents	702	701.9550
pure major third, in cents	386	386.3137
pythagorean comma, in cents	24	23.4600
syntonic comma, in cents	22	21.5063
−1/4 PC, in cents	−6	−5.865
fifth −1/4 PC, in cents	696	696.090
fifth −1/4 PC freq. ratio	1.4949	1.494926964
−1/4 SC, in cents	−5.5	−5.376575
fifth −1/4 SC, in cents	696.5	696.578425
fifth −1/4 SC freq. ratio	1.4953	1.49534878
−1/5 PC, in cents	−4.8	−4.692
fifth −1/5 PC, in cents	697.2	697.263
fifth −1/5 PC freq. ratio	1.4959	1.495940197
−1/6 PC, in cents	−4	−3.91
fifth −1/6 PC, in cents	698	698.045
fifth −1/6 PC freq. ratio	1.4966	1.496616067
−1/6 SC, in cents	−3.7	−3.584383
fifth −1/6 SC, in cents	698.3	698.37062
fifth −1/6 SC freq. ratio	1.4969	1.496897583
−1/12 PC, in cents	−2	−1.955
fifth −1/12 PC, in cents	700	700.000
fifth −1/12 PC freq. ratio	1.4984	1.498307079

cents, the key sequence on the calculator is: 696.090, ÷, 3986.3137, =, 10^X. This gives the answer 1.494926964. Of course, for the pure fifths with a precise cent value of 701.955, the frequency ratio is 1.5. The results are given in table 4.3.

Table 4.2. Precise Cent Values of Werckmeister III Fifths

Interval	Cents	Interval	Cents
C–G	696.090	F♯–C♯	701.955
G–D	696.090	C♯–G♯	701.955
D–A	696.090	G♯–E♭	701.955
A–E	701.955	E♭–B♭	701.955
E–B	701.955	B♭–F	701.955
B–F♯	696.090	F–C	701.955

Table 4.3. Precise Frequency Ratios of Werckmeister III Fifths

Interval	F.R.	Interval	F.R.
C–G	1.494926964	F♯–C♯	1.5
G–D	1.494926964	C♯–G♯	1.5
D–A	1.494926964	G♯–E♭	1.5
A–E	1.5	E♭–B♭	1.5
E–B	1.5	B♭–F	1.5
B–F♯	1.494926964	F–C	1.5

Next, the frequencies are calculated for each of the notes from c to b. The general procedure is as follows. We start at the reference note of a and proceed "down" the list of note names in the circle of fifths: a, e, b, $f\#$, $c\#$, and so on. (Some representations of the circle of fifths are actually circles, so this progression is considered "clockwise.") The known frequency is multiplied by the appropriate frequency ratio— which in Werckmeister III is either 1.5 for the pure fifths or 1.494926964 for the tempered fifths—to obtain the frequency of the next note. Then the result is divided by 2 if the frequency goes above the tenor octave; that is, if the frequency exceeds roughly 261 Hz.

The pitch reference to be used is A440. This means $a^1 = 440$ Hz and $a = 220$ Hz. (Further discussion of pitch levels is given in chapter 8.) From a, we first find the frequency of e, a fourth below a. Multiply 220—the frequency of a—by 1.5—the frequency ratio of the Werckmeister fifth A–E taken from the table 4.3—to get the answer 330 Hz. This is the frequency of e^{l}, a fifth above a and an octave higher than we need. Divide this result by 2, and this gives the frequency of e, **165.0000** Hz. To maintain the precision of the calculations, the frequencies will be given to the fourth decimal place. When the series of calculations are done on a calculator, simply use whatever value the calculator returns, even if it is more than four decimal places.

From e = 165.0000 Hz, multiply by 1.5 (the frequency ratio of the fifth E–B) to get the frequency of b, a fifth above e: **247.5000** Hz.

To obtain the frequency of $f\#$ from b, the calculations are:

$$
\begin{array}{cccc}
 & \text{B–F}\sharp & & \\
b & \text{freq. ratio} & f\#^{l} & f\# \\
247.5000 & \times \ 1.494926964 & = 369.9944 \div 2 = & \mathbf{184.9972} \ \text{Hz.}
\end{array}
$$

Again, multiplying by the frequency ratio gives the frequency a fifth above b, so we divide by 2. To continue:

$c\#$:	184.9972 × 1.5 = 277.4958 ÷ 2 = **138.7479** Hz;
$g\#$:	138.7479 × 1.5 = **208.1219** Hz;
$e\flat$:	208.1219 × 1.5 = 312.1828 ÷ 2 = **156.0914** Hz;
$b\flat$:	156.0914 × 1.5 = **234.1371** Hz;
f:	234.1371 × 1.5 = 351.2056 ÷ 2 = **175.6028** Hz;
c:	175.6028 × 1.5 = 263.4042 ÷ 2 = **131.7021** Hz;
g:	131.7021 × 1.494926964 = **196.8850** Hz;
d:	196.8850 × 1.494926964 = 294.3288 ÷ 2 = **147.1644** Hz.

The complete list of Werckmeister III frequencies is given in table 4.4.

One stops the calculations at d and does not calculate a from d, since a was the starting note. Here we can demonstrate the advantage of using the precise values. If the frequency of a was calculated from the frequency of d, we would get

$$147.1644 \times 1.494926964 = 220.0000.$$

This demonstrates that the calculations "close" the circle of fifths properly and the circle is mathematically correct.

We may also use the same procedure starting from c. If we were calculating the frequencies for meantone temperament, it would be a

Table 4.4. Werckmeister III Frequencies, Tenor Octave

Note	Frequency	Note	Frequency
c	131.7021 Hz	f♯	184.9972 Hz
c♯	138.7479	g	196.8850
d	147.1644	g♯	208.1219
e♭	156.0914	a	220.0000
e	165.0000	b♭	234.1371
f	175.6028	b	247.5000

slightly different procedure in order to avoid the wolf interval G♯–E♭. First, we would calculate a, e, b, $f♯$, $c♯$, and $g♯$ as above, multiplying the frequencies by the frequency ratio of the fifth and dividing by 2 as necessary. Then, we would start at a again and proceed in the other direction—d, g, c, f, $b♭$, and $e♭$—which would involve *dividing* the frequencies by the frequency ratio of the fifth and *multiplying* by 2 as necessary to keep the results in the tenor octave.

Tables 4.9 through 4.12 at the end of the chapter present worksheets that may be helpful in calculating frequencies.

Calculating Beat Rates

Using the frequencies in table 4.4, we can now calculate the beat rates for Werckmeister III.

General Procedure

1. Select the type of interval: fifth, fourth, major third, minor third, or major sixth.

2. Identify the frequency ratio of the interval: 3:2 for a fifth, 4:3 for a fourth, 5:4 for a major third, 6:5 for a minor third, or 5:3 for a major sixth. Notice that it is the frequency ratio of the *pure* interval.

3. Select the two frequencies in the interval.

4. Calculate the coinciding harmonic frequencies by multiplying the frequencies of the notes by the ratio numbers according to the following protocol:

Interval	Lower Note Multiplied by	Upper Note Multiplied by
fifth	3	2
fourth	4	3
major third	5	4
minor third	6	5
major sixth	5	3

5. Subtract the lower-note product from the upper-note product. This is the number of beats per second. A negative sign denotes an interval narrower than pure and a positive number denotes an interval wider than pure.

Example No. 1

selected interval: the fifth *c–g*, frequency ratio 3:2
frequency of *c*: 131.7021 Hz; frequency of *g*: 196.8850 Hz c
coinciding harmonic frequency for *c*: 131.7021 × 3 = 395.1063
coinciding harmonic frequency for *g*: 196.8850 × 2 = 393.7700
difference: 393.7700 − 395.1063 = −1.3 beats per second

Example No. 2

selected interval: the fourth *c–f*, frequency ratio 4:3
frequency of *c*: 131.7021 Hz; frequency of *f*: 175.6028 Hz
coinciding harmonic frequency for *c*: 131.7021 × 4 = 526.8084
coinciding harmonic frequency for *f*: 175.6028 × 3 = 526.8084
difference: 526.8084 − 526.8084 = 0 beats per second

Example No. 3

selected interval: the major third *c–e*, frequency ratio 5:4
frequency of *c*: 131.7021 Hz; frequency of *e*: 165.0000 Hz
coinciding harmonic frequency for *c*: 131.7021 × 5 = 658.5105
coinciding harmonic frequency for *e*: 165.0000 × 4 = 660.0000
difference: 660.0000 − 658.5105 = +1.5 beats per second

When calculating beats for some notes you will need frequencies above *b*, which may be determined from the list already calculated. For example, for the fifth on *g* you will need the frequency of *d¹*. This is obtained by multiplying the frequency of *d* by 2.

An alternate method of beat calculation is given below. Equations that relate beat rates and frequencies are also given below.

Table 4.5 gives the beat rates for fifths, fourths, and major thirds in the tenor octave for Werckmeister III, rounded to one decimal place. Beat rates for other temperaments are given in chapter 12. For some temperaments, it may also be helpful to calculate beat rates for major sixths and minor thirds.

Table 4.5. Beat Rates for Werckmeister III

Note	Fifths	Fourths	Major Thirds
c	−1.3	0	1.5
c#	0	0	8.7
d	−1.5	2.0	4.2
e♭	0	0	7.1
e	0	0	7.5
f	0	0	2.0
f#	0	2.5	11.6
g	−2.0	2.7	5.6
g#	0	0	13.0
a	0	3.0	10.0
b♭	0	0	6.6
b	−2.5	0	11.2

Equations Relating Beat Rates and Frequencies

The general procedure for calculating beat rates from frequencies may be presented in the form of equations (table 4.6). These equations may also be used to calculate a frequency when the beat rate and one frequency are known. The abbreviations may be understood as follows: "B.R." refers to the beat rate; the intervals of a fifth, fourth, major third, minor third, and major sixth are abbreviated 5, 4, M3, m3, and M6, respectively; "$f_{\uparrow 5}$" refers to the upper frequency in a fifth interval; "$f_{\downarrow 5}$" refers to the lower frequency in a fifth interval; "$f_{\uparrow M3}$" refers to the upper frequency in a major third interval; and so on.

Table 4.6. Equations Relating Beat Rates and Frequencies

Fifth	Fourth
$B.R._5 = 2(f_{\uparrow 5}) - 3(f_{\downarrow 5})$	$B.R._4 = 3(f_{\uparrow 4}) - 4(f_{\downarrow 4})$
$f_{\uparrow 5} = \dfrac{B.R._5 + 3(f_{\downarrow 5})}{2}$	$f_{\uparrow 4} = \dfrac{B.R._4 + 4(f_{\downarrow 4})}{3}$
$f_{\downarrow 5} = \dfrac{2(f_{\uparrow 5}) - B.R._5}{3}$	$f_{\downarrow 4} = \dfrac{3(f_{\uparrow 4}) - B.R._4}{4}$

Major Third	Minor Third
$B.R._{M3} = 4(f_{\uparrow M3}) - 5(f_{\downarrow M3})$	$B.R._{m3} = 5(f_{\uparrow m3}) - 6(f_{\downarrow m3})$
$f_{\uparrow M3} = \dfrac{B.R._{M3} + 5(f_{\downarrow M3})}{4}$	$f_{\uparrow m3} = \dfrac{B.R._{m3} + 6(f_{\downarrow m3})}{5}$
$f_{\downarrow M3} = \dfrac{4(f_{\uparrow M3}) - B.R._{M3}}{5}$	$f_{\downarrow m3} = \dfrac{5(f_{\uparrow m3}) - B.R._{m3}}{6}$

Major Sixth
$B.R._{M6} = 3(f_{\uparrow M6}) - 5(f_{\downarrow M6})$
$f_{\uparrow M6} = \dfrac{B.R._{M6} + 5(f_{\downarrow M6})}{3}$
$f_{\downarrow M6} = \dfrac{3(f_{\uparrow M6}) - B.R._{M6}}{5}$

Alternate Pitch References

The frequencies in table 4.4 and the beat rates in table 4.5 were calculated based on a pitch reference of A440. One could also do the calculations using other pitch references, such as A392, A415, or A466. If one set of values has already been calculated, it is easy to convert the existing values to another pitch reference simply by multiplying by a conversion factor. The conversion factor is determined by dividing the new pitch level by 440 and multiplying each note's frequency by that factor to get a new frequency. Likewise, you can multiply each interval's beat rate by the same conversion factor and get a new beat rate. Conversion factors for several possible situations are given in table 4.7.

Table 4.7. Conversion Factors for Alternate Pitch References

Direction	Example	Multiply by
up two semitones	A392 to A440	1.1224621
up one semitone	A415 to A440	1.0594631
down one semitone	A440 to A415	0.9438743
down two semitones	A440 to A392	0.8908987

For example, the frequency of g in Werckmeister III is 196.8850 Hz at A440, as given in table 4.4. The frequency of g at A415—down one semitone—would be

$$196.8850 \times 0.9438743 = 185.8347 \text{ Hz.}$$

The beat rate of g–d^l in Werckmeister III at A440 is –2.0, as given in table 4.5. The beat rate at A415 would be

$$-2.0 \times 0.9438743 = -1.89 \text{ beats per second.}$$

For atypical pitch references, use the same approach; for example, for a pitch reference of 403 Hz, the conversion factor is $403 \div 440 = 0.91591$. Pitch references are discussed further in chapter 8.

Tuning and Tempering Steps

Now we look for certain features in the list of the fifths (table 4.2) and in the beat rates (table 4.5) that may be easily translated into tuning and tempering instructions. The following general elements may be noted: (1) pure intervals, particularly fifths, fourths, and major thirds; (2) beat rates between 2 and 6 beats per second, especially if they are whole numbers (beat rates below 2 are sometimes difficult to hear, and beat rates over 6 are difficult to count properly); and (3) intervals with identical or similar beat rates that may be compared with one another. These elements with respect to Werckmeister III are: (1) the six consecutive pure fifths F#–C#, C#–G#, G#–E♭, E♭–B♭, and B♭–F, plus two additional adjacent pure fifths on A–E and E–B; (2) whole-number beat rates of d–g, g–d^l, and f–a with 2 beats per second; and (3) identical beat rates of the third c–e (+1.5) with the fifth d–a (–1.5), as well as d–g (+2.0), g–d^l (–2.0), and f–a (+2.0) mentioned above. Concerning these last examples, while it is important to temper narrow or wide intervals correctly, there is actually no difference whether the interval is narrower than pure or wider than pure with respect to counting beats. That is, an interval tempered +2.0 will beat the same as an interval tempered –2.0.

All we need to do to tie these elements together is to find a way to connect them with the starting note—typically C or A—and then be sure that we account for all twelve chromatic notes from c to b.

Begin by looking at the intervals which contain the starting note A. Intervals that include an a and their beat rates are:

$$d–a \qquad –1.5 \quad \text{beats per second;}$$
$$e–a \qquad 0 \quad \text{beats per second;}$$
$$f–a \qquad +2.0 \quad \text{beats per second.}$$

Of these, the fifth d–a will be the least useful because of the fractional beat rate. After setting a to pitch, e is tuned pure to a, and b is tuned pure to e. Then f is set so that the major third f–a is tempered wider than pure at 2 beats per second. From f, the following notes are tuned as pure fifths and fourths: c, $b♭$, $e♭$, $g\#$, $c\#$, and $f\#$. At this point ten notes would be set, leaving d and g. Each of these last two notes is now considered with respect to the intervals it is a part of, and the corresponding beat rates are reviewed.

d: *d–f♯* (+4.2) *g*: *c–g* (–1.3)
    d–g (+2.0)   *e♭–g* (+7.1)
    d–a (–1.5)   *g–b* (+5.6)
               g–c¹ (+2.7)
               g–d¹ (–2.0)

From this information, one could set *g* by tempering *c–g* narrower than pure slightly more than 1 beat per second, then set *d* by tempering *d–g* wider than pure 2 beats per second. Another approach would be to set *d* by tempering *d–a* narrower than pure so that it beats just like *c–e* (–1.5 vs +1.5), then setting *g* by tempering *d–g* wider than pure 2 beats per second. The second approach is probably easier.

Many instructions for setting a temperament also include tests or checks to be sure the tempering steps are correct. Usually such checks entail comparing the beat rates between two different intervals. For example, once *d* and *g* are set, one may check *d–g* (+2.0) against *f–a* (+2.0). Checks are more important for temperaments that have many tempering steps.

The same process is used for generating a set of tuning instructions starting from C. In this case, once *c* and *c¹* are tuned to the proper pitch level, *f* may be tuned pure to *c*. With *f* tuned, one can temper *f–a* wider than pure 2 beats per second and tune *b♭*, *e♭*, *g♯*, *c♯*, and *f♯* in a series of pure fifths and fourths. Then *e* is tuned pure to *a*, and *b* is tuned pure to *e*. Finally, *d* and *g* are set in one of the two ways mentioned above. Complete instructions for setting a variety of temperaments are given in chapter 6.

For some temperaments, major sixths and even minor thirds may need to be taken into account when generating tuning instructions.

The above procedure produces what has been called the *theoretically correct method*. Another approach is the *equal-beating method*. These terms have been used by Owen Jorgensen.[1] The theoretically correct method uses beat rates to set the tempered intervals. Since beat rates are calculated from the actual frequencies, which in turn are determined from the frequency ratios and cent values of the fifths, this method is closely related to the mathematical representation of a temperament. The equal-beating method does not use the calculated beat rates; rather, two different intervals are tempered to beat at the same rate, even though this deviates from the cent values of the intervals. For example, in Werckmeister III, the major thirds *B♭–d* and *d–f♯* are the same size (396 cents; see table 2.4). However, their beat rates are different; d–$f\sharp$ has a higher beat rate than $B\flat$–d (+4.2 vs. +3.3; see table 4.5) because d has a higher frequency than $B\flat$, and $f\sharp$ has a higher frequency than d. Using the theoretically correct method, this difference in beat rate would be maintained. Using the equal-beating method, d would be tuned between $B\flat$ and $f\sharp$ so that the two major thirds beat at the same rate, without having to calculate that rate. The advantages of an equal-beating method are that it is often easier to set and requires no knowledge of specific beat rates.[2] A discussion of theoretical vs. equal-beating versions is given in chapter 9.

To develop an equal-beating version, we need to have a theoretically correct version already at hand, as given above. Identify the notes that cannot be tuned pure to other notes but require some sort of tempering; in Werckmeister III, these would be the notes d, f, and g. Evaluate the intervals that include these notes.

d:		f:		g:	
$B\flat$–d	(+3.3)	$c\sharp$–f	(+8.7)	d–g	(+2.0)
d–$f\sharp$	(+4.2)	f–a	(+2.0)	$e\flat$–g	(+7.1)
d–g	(+2.0)	f–$b\flat$	(0)	g–b	(+5.6)
d–a	(−1.5)	f–c^{l}	(0)	g–c^{l}	(+2.7)
				g–d^{l}	(−2.0)

Since the major third f–a is wider than pure at exactly 2 beats per second and since it relates to the a pitch reference, we will forego changing any f-related intervals. Next we eliminate those intervals from the list whose beat rates are not close enough to any others, such as $e\flat$–g and g–b. The following intervals remain.

d:		g:	
$B\flat$–d	(+3.3)	d–g	(+2.0)
d–$f\sharp$	(+4.2)	g–c^{l}	(+2.7)
d–g	(+2.0)	g–d^{l}	(−2.0)
d–a	(−1.5)		

Now we look for a pair of intervals for each of the notes in question—d and g—which have similar beat rates. For d, $B\flat$–d and d–$f\sharp$ have close beat rates, and for g, d–g and g–c^{l} may be used. The $B\flat$–d–$f\sharp$ intervals were discussed earlier. The note g could be tuned equidistant from d and c^{l} so that d–g and g–c^{l} beat at the same rate, which need not be calculated. This technique is described in chapter 5.

Alternate Method of Calculating Beat Rates

General Procedure

This method is based in the work of Rudolf Rasch.[3]

1. Select the desired interval and its cent value.
2. Determine the frequency ratio of the tempered interval. This may be calculated from the cent value using the equation

$$\text{frequency ratio} = 10^{(\text{cent value} \div 3986.3137)}$$

3. Divide the frequency ratio of the tempered interval by the decimal equivalent of the frequency ratio of its pure counterpart:

fifth	1.50	minor third	1.20
fourth	1.33 . . .	major sixth	1.66 . . .
major third	1.25		

4. Take the natural logarithm (ln or $\log_e$) of the value found in the preceding step, and multiply the result by the higher number in the interval's frequency ratio (3 for a fifth, 4 for a fourth, 5 for a third, etc.).
5. The result is called the *relative beat frequency*. Multiplying any frequency by the relative beat frequency yields the beat rate for that class of interval at that particular frequency. If there are different sizes of, say, fifths in a temperament, each different size has its own relative beat frequency.

Example No. 1

1. selected interval: a fifth narrowed by one-quarter of the syntonic comma, with a precise value of 696.578425 cents
2. frequency ratio $= 10^{(696.578425 \div 3986.3137)} = 1.49534878$
(Using a scientific calculator, the key sequence for this calculation is: 696.578425, $\div$, 3986.3137, =, 10^X.)
3. relative frequency ratio: $1.49534878 \div 1.5 = 0.996899186$
4. relative beat frequency: $\ln(0.996899186) \times 3 = -0.009316891$

5. If c^l = 261.6 Hz, the beat rate of a fifth tempered narrower than pure by one-quarter of the syntonic comma (696.578425 cents) with c^l as the lower note in the interval is

261.6 × –0.009316891 = –2.4 beats per second.

The negative sign indicates an interval narrower than pure.

Example No. 2

1. selected interval: a major third in equal temperament, 400 cents
2. frequency ratio = $10^{(400 \div 3986.3137)}$ = 1.259921051
(Using a scientific calculator, the key sequence for this calculation is: 400, ÷, 3986.3137, =, 10^X.)
3. relative frequency ratio: 1.259921051 ÷ 1.25 = 1.007936841
4. relative beat frequency: ln(1.007936841) × 5 = 0.039527548
5. If c = 130.8 Hz, the beat rate of a major third wider than pure as in equal temperament with c as the lower note in the interval would be

130.8 × 0.039527548 = +5.2 beats per second.

The positive sign indicates an interval wider than pure.

Derivation of Precise Values

Cent Equation Constant

The value of the constant 3986.3137 used in the cent equation is calculated from the expression 1200 ÷ log 2 (see chapter 11).

Pure Fifth

The cent value of a pure fifth is calculated using the cent equation, the precise value for the constant, and a value of 1.5 for the frequency ratio:

cent value = 3986.3137 × log (1.5) = 701.9550.

Pure Major Third

The cent value of a pure major third is calculated by using the cent equation, the precise value for the constant, and a value of 1.25 for the frequency ratio:

cent value = 3986.3137 × log (1.25) = 386.3137.

Pythagorean Comma

The cent value of the Pythagorean comma is calculated by subtracting the product of seven pure octaves from the product of twelve pure fifths, using the precise cent value for a pure fifth:

(12 × 701.9550) − (7 × 1200) = 23.4600.

Syntonic Comma

The cent value of the syntonic comma is calculated by adding the value of four pure fifths using the precise value, subtracting the value of two pure octaves (which gives the value of a Pythagorean third), and then subtracting the precise value of a pure major third:

(4 × 701.9550) − (2 × 1200) − 386.3137 = 21.5063.

Fifth Tempering

The fifth tempering shown in table 4.1 is given in three ways: as a portion of the Pythagorean comma, as the cent value of the fifth, and as the frequency ratio of the fifth.

Comma. The portion of the comma representing −1/4 SC is calculated by dividing the precise value of the syntonic comma by 4:

21.5063 ÷ 4 = 5.376575.

For −1/6 PC:

23.4600 ÷ 6 = 3.91.

A negative sign is added to denote an interval narrower than pure.

Size of Fifth. The cent value of a tempered fifth is obtained by subtracting the comma tempering from the value of a pure fifth. For a fifth tempered –1/4 SC:

$$701.9550 - 5.376575 = 696.578425.$$

For a fifth tempered –1/6 PC:

$$701.9550 - 3.91 = 698.045.$$

Frequency Ratio. The frequency ratio of a tempered fifth is calculated using the rearranged version of the cent equation, the precise value for the constant, and the precise value of the fifth in cents. For a fifth tempered –1/4 SC:

$$\text{frequency ratio} = 10^{(696.578425 \div 3986.3137)} = 1.49534878.$$

For a fifth tempered –1/6 PC:

$$\text{frequency ratio} = 10^{(698.045 \div 3986.3137)} = 1.496616067.$$

Temperament Units

An alternate way to characterize the size of an interval instead of cents is in terms of *temperament units* (TU).[4] This approach was invented by the organbuilder John Brombaugh. Temperament units can be added and subtracted like cents, but since there are 30 TU to 1 cent, decimals and fractional values are avoided. Another advantage is that the TU values for both commas are divisible by 3, 4, 5, 6, and 12 without remainder, making calculations simpler. However, the use of cents tends to be more widespread. The relationship of TU to cents is given in table 4.8.

Table 4.8. Temperament Units (TU)

Name	Cent Value	TU Value
schisma, 1/12 PC	2	60
1/6 SC	3.67	110
1/6 PC	4	120
1/5 PC	4.8	144
1/4 SC	5.5	165
1/4 PC	6	180
syntonic comma	22	660
Pythagorean comma	24	720

Sources of Confusion

Equal Size vs. Equal-Beating

Two intervals may either be the same size—that is, have the same cent value—or have the same beat rate, but not both. In other words, equal size does not mean equal-beating. The size of an interval in cents is derived from that interval's frequency ratio, which is independent of the actual frequencies. On the other hand, a beat rate is the difference between coinciding harmonic frequencies, which are dependent on the actual fundamental frequencies of the notes in the interval. As mentioned above, in Werckmeister III the two major thirds $B\flat$–d and d–$f\#$ have the same cent values, but the beat rate of d–$f\#$ would be faster than the beat rate of $B\flat$–d because the frequencies in the d–$f\#$ interval are higher. If one were to temper those two intervals so they have the same beat rate, you would have to make $B\flat$–d narrower or make d–$f\#$ wider, changing their size and therefore their cent values.

Another example is the situation in which any major third is derived from four fifths of equal size—for example, the C–E interval in all the temperaments mentioned in chapter 2 except Werckmeister III and Sorge. In terms of cent values, each of the fifths C–G, G–D, D–A, and A–E are the same size for the following temperaments: –1/4 SC for 1/4-comma meantone, Kirnberger III, and Rameau; –1/5 PC for *tempérament ordinaire* and Kellner; –1/6 SC for 1/6-comma meantone; and –1/6 PC for Vallotti, Young nos. 1 and 2, Neidhardt, Barnes, and

Lindley. As a result, one will sometimes find tuning instructions that say either to tune the interval C–E pure or to temper it to specific beat rate, then "temper the four constituent fifths equally." This is ambiguous, because it may be taken to mean *either* equal size according to exact (and different) beat rates *or* the same beat rate, which ends up deviating from exact cent values. Either approach is acceptable, but the difference should be appreciated. If *c–g* and *d–a* are tempered to equal cent size, *d–a* beats faster than *c–g* because *d* and *a* have higher frequencies than *c* and *g*. On the other hand, if they are tempered to the same beat rates, the cent values are not the same.

Equal-Beating Method vs. Equal-Beating Intervals

The equal-beating *method* of setting a temperament refers to the tempering of different intervals to the same beat rate that otherwise would have different beat rates in the theoretically correct version of the same temperament. This should not be confused with equal-beating *intervals*, which are intervals that just happen to have identical beat rates in the theoretically correct version. For example, *d–g* and *f–a* in Werckmeister III are both wider than pure at 2.0 beats per second (table 4.4).

Summary

The procedure for generating a set of tuning instructions for a temperament involves the following steps:

1. obtain a list of the cent values of the fifths;
2. calculate the frequency ratios of the fifths;
3. calculate the actual frequencies for the twelve chromatic notes in the tenor octave, from *c* to *b*;
4. calculate the beat rates for the fifths, fourths, and major thirds for the twelve chromatic notes from *c* to *b*;
5. identify features of the fifth intervals and the beat rates that may be easily translated into tuning and tempering instructions, such as pure intervals, whole-number beat rates between 2 and 6 beats per second, and similar beat rates that may be compared;
6. relate the elements in (5) to the starting note;

7. for the notes that are not easily set, inspect all the intervals of which they are a part, and consider using equal-beating intervals;

8. account for all twelve chromatic notes from c to b.

Precise values are recommended for calculating beat rates so that the circle of fifths is correctly represented mathematically.

Table 4.9. Worksheet for Calculating Frequencies c to b for a Temperament with No Wolf Interval, "A" Pitch Reference

_____ × _____ = _____ ÷ 2 = _____
    a freq. ratio A–E e^l e

× _____ = _____
   freq. ratio E–B b

× _____ = _____ ÷ 2 = _____
   freq. ratio B–F♯ $f\sharp^l$ $f\sharp$

× _____ = _____ ÷ 2 = _____
   freq. ratio F♯–C♯ $c\sharp^l$ $c\sharp$

× _____ = _____
   freq. ratio C♯–G♯ $g\sharp$

× _____ = _____ ÷ 2 = _____
   freq. ratio G♯–E♭ $e\flat^l$ $e\flat$

× _____ = _____
   freq. ratio E♭–B♭ $b\flat$

× _____ = _____ ÷ 2 = _____
   freq. ratio B♭–F f^l f

× _____ = _____ ÷ 2 = _____
   freq. ratio F–C c^l c

× _____ = _____
   freq. ratio C–G g

× _____ = _____ ÷ 2 = _____
   freq. ratio G–D d^l d

Table 4.10. Worksheet for Calculating Frequencies c to b for a Temperament with No Wolf Interval, "C" Pitch Reference

_____ × _____ = _____
c freq. ratio C–G g

× _____ = _____ ÷ 2 = _____
freq. ratio G–D d^l d

× _____ = _____
freq. ratio D–A a

× _____ = _____ ÷ 2 = _____
freq. ratio A–E e^l e

× _____ = _____
freq. ratio E–B b

× _____ = _____ ÷ 2 = _____
freq. ratio B–F♯ $f\sharp^l$ $f\sharp$

× _____ = _____ ÷ 2 = _____
freq. ratio F♯–C♯ $c\sharp^l$ $c\sharp$

)(_____ = _____
freq. ratio C♯–G♯ $g\sharp$

× _____ = _____ ÷ 2 = _____
freq. ratio G♯–E♭ $e♭^l$ $e♭$

× _____ = _____
freq. ratio E♭–B♭ $b♭$

× _____ = _____ ÷ 2 = _____
freq. ratio B♭–F f^l f

Table 4.11. Worksheet for Calculating Frequencies c to b for a Temperament with a Wolf Interval at G♯–E♭, "A" Pitch Reference

_____ a	× _____ freq. ratio A–E	= _____ e^l	÷ 2 =	_____ e
	× _____ freq. ratio E–B		=	_____ b
	× _____ freq. ratio B–F♯	= _____ $f\#^l$	÷ 2 =	_____ $f\#$
	× _____ freq. ratio F♯–C♯	= _____ $c\#^l$	÷ 2 =	_____ $c\#$
	× _____ freq. ratio C♯–G♯		=	_____ $g\#$
_____ a	÷ _____ freq. ratio D–A		=	_____ d
	÷ _____ freq. ratio G–D	= _____ G	× 2 =	_____ g
	÷ _____ freq. ratio C–G		=	_____ c
	÷ _____ freq. ratio F–C	= _____ F	× 2 =	_____ f
	÷ _____ freq. ratio B♭–F	= _____ $B\flat$	× 2 =	_____ $b\flat$
	÷ _____ freq. ratio E♭–B♭		=	_____ $e\flat$

Table 4.12. Worksheet for Calculating Frequencies c to b for a Temperament with a Wolf Interval at G♯–E♭, "C" Pitch Reference

---

_____ × _____   = _____
c freq. ratio C–G g

× _____ = _____ ÷ 2 = _____
  freq. ratio G–D d^l d

× _____   = _____
  freq. ratio D–A a

× _____ = _____ ÷ 2 = _____
  freq. ratio A–E e^l e

× _____   = _____
  freq. ratio E–B b

× _____ = _____ ÷ 2 = _____
  freq. ratio B–F♯ $f\sharp^l$ $f\sharp$

× _____ = _____ ÷ 2 = _____
  freq. ratio F♯–C♯ $c\sharp^l$ $c\sharp$

× _____   = _____
  freq. ratio C♯–G♯ $g\sharp$

_____ ÷ _____ = _____ × 2 = _____
c freq. ratio F–C F f

÷ _____ = _____ × 2 = _____
  freq. ratio B♭–F $B\flat$ $b\flat$

÷ _____   = _____
  freq. ratio E♭–B♭ $e\flat$

Notes

1. Owen Jorgensen, *Tuning the Historical Temperaments by Ear* (Marquette: Northern Michigan University Press, 1977), 9–11, 419, 429.

2. Jorgensen, *Tuning the Historical Temperaments*, 9–10.

3. Rudolf Rasch, "Theory of Helmholtz-Beat Frequencies," *Music Perception* 1 (Spring 1984): 308–22.

4. Bradley Lehman, "Bach's Extraordinary Temperament: Our Rosetta Stone–1." *Early Music* 33 (February 2005): 5.

5

The Tuning Process

With respect to the stringed keyboard instruments—harpsichord, clavichord, and fortepiano—the *tuning process* refers to all the steps involved in adjusting each string in the instrument to its proper pitch. This process consists of three stages. First, one tunes a note to a reference pitch. Second, one tunes and tempers a series of intervals so that the other eleven notes in the chromatic scale are brought to their respective pitches according to a given plan. This is called *laying the bearings*. Third, one tunes all other notes to these bearings by unisons and octaves. The first two parts of the tuning process are detailed for each temperament in a set of tuning instructions, which are presented in chapter 6. The present chapter will discuss selected procedures and techniques—the "mechanics"—involved in the tuning process. The skills needed include using a tuning fork, using a tuning tool, listening for beats, setting intervals pure and to specific beat rates, and keeping oriented. This material is a compilation based on the author's experience and several published sources.[1]

Tuning Fork

The number of tuning forks you will need may vary. If you only perform for yourself at home, keep your instrument at only one pitch level, and always set your selected temperaments from the note C, you will only need one tuning fork. For other circumstances, you will probably need more than one. The four most commonly used tuning forks follow:

G♯415.3 for A at A415   B493.9 for C at A415

A440.0 for A at A440   C523.3 for C at A440

It should be noted that most tuning forks are based on equal temperament frequencies.

Position your hand—whichever hand does not use the tuning
tool—palm-side up, and place the handle of the tuning fork between
your index and middle fingers with the tuning fork upside down. Stabi-
lize the fork with your thumb and strike the tines of the fork against the
heel of your shoe or your knee. Release your thumb from the stem of
the fork and place the stem against the underside of the instrument near
the key you need to depress. Use your thumb to depress the key. This
leaves your other hand free to use the tuning tool.

Once the reference string is set, if you wish you may strike the
fork, hold it up to your ear, play the string, and compare the pitches.

Tuning Tool

There are two main varieties of tuning tools. One is T-shaped and is
usually referred to as a tuning wrench or key, while the other has a long
"gooseneck" handle and is called a tuning hammer. Make sure the tool
is seated all the way down on the tuning pin. When using the tool, you
should always have a sense that you are *rotating* the tuning pin, not
tipping or bending it. The motion of rotating the pin is very slow. After
the string is tuned, gently remove the tool from the pin. The pitch of the
string should always be double-checked after the tool has been removed to be sure that removal of the tool did not change the pitch.

String Movement

During the tuning process, use as little movement of the tuning tool as
possible. Changing a string's pitch makes the string rub up against the
wood of the nut and bridge, as well as against their respective pins. The
tuning pin also abrades the wrestplank. All these contact points wear
the materials involved. Since stringed keyboard instruments are tuned a
great many times during their lives, minimal movement while tuning is
suggested.

Many people recommend lowering the pitch of the string slightly
and then bringing the string up to the proper pitch. This offers an audible clue that you are on the correct tuning pin. If you are playing a C on

the keyboard but are unknowingly turning the tuning pin for the adjacent C♯ string, the continual raising of the pitch will eventually cause the string to break, with no warning to you. The initial lowering of the pitch may also help to equalize the tension among the three sections of the string—tuning pin to nut pin, nut pin to bridge pin, bridge pin to hitchpin—and may produce a more stable tuning.

To assure one has the tuning tool on the proper tuning pin, play the string from the keyboard and then touch the vibrating string with your finger or the end of the tuning tool to verify which string is vibrating. Then follow the string to the correct tuning pin.

Listening for Beats

Other than tuning the very first note to the tuning fork, setting a temperament involves playing two notes simultaneously and either tuning the interval pure or tempering it to a certain degree. Either way, you are listening for beats.

Listening for beats involves two things. First, ignore the two notes themselves and listen to the interval as a whole. You are not interested in the loudness, timbre, attack, decay, or any other aspect of the individual notes. You are listening to their interaction: either the presence of beats caused by the difference in the coinciding harmonic frequencies or the absence of beats. Second, focus your attention at the pitch where the coinciding harmonic frequencies are located; this is where beats occur (table 5.1).

Table 5.1. Location of Beats for Selected Intervals

Interval	Example	Location of Beats	Example
unison	c–c	at the unison	c
octave	c–c^1	at the top note	c^1
fifth	c–g	one octave above top note	g^1
fourth	c–f	two octaves above lower note	c^2
major third	c–e	two octaves above top note	e^2
minor third	c–e^b	two octaves above missing 5th	g^2
major sixth	c–a	two octaves above missing 3rd	e^2

Start by tuning unisons, which is easy to do on a harpsichord with two eight-foot registers. If your instrument does not have two eight-foot registers, begin by tuning octaves, as described below. For the clavichord and fortepiano with multiple unisons per key, you need to mute the third unison string if present. Play c (tenor C), and lower the pitch of one string so that they are out of tune. Non-pure, out-of-tune unisons sound dissonant, rough, or coarse. Now raise the pitch of the lowered string, and listen carefully for the wavering in the sound that indicates beats. Re-play the note every few seconds to keep it sounding, ignoring the initial attack and concentrating on the main sound. As you bring the unisons closer to pitch, the undulations get slower until they are actually quite pleasant. Slow beats are responsible for the *chorus effect*, which is a mild wavering in pitch often heard in choral groups or in string orchestras. Organists know this as the *céleste* effect. Continue raising the pitch of the string until there is a point at which the wavering disappears and the two individual tones seem to coalesce into a single sound. This is a pure, beatless unison. Repeat this exercise until you can hear beats and tune a pure unison easily.

Next, tune the octave c–c^1. On a harpsichord, use one register; on a clavichord or fortepiano, mute all strings but one for each of the c and c^1 keys. Leave c alone, and turn the tuning pin for the c^1 string. Lower its pitch to create the rough out-of-tuneness, then raise its pitch, and listen carefully. Focus your attention on the pitch of the upper note, replaying the c–c^1 interval every few seconds and ignoring the initial attack. Raise the pitch of c^1, listen for beats, and notice how the beat rate can be controlled by the tuning tool. When you lower the pitch of c^1 and make the octave narrower than pure, you can increase the beat rate; when you raise the pitch toward pure, you can decrease the rate. So, if you have trouble hearing the beats initially, increase and decrease the beat rate so the beats become more evident to you. (A note of caution: tuning an interval *wider* than pure will increase the beat rate in the same way as tuning an interval narrower than pure. If you mistakenly believe an interval is narrower than pure but it is wider than pure and you continue to raise the pitch, the string will break. Always be aware of "where" the pure interval is so you can tell if a tempered interval is narrower or wider than pure.) Play the c^1 note by itself once in a while to remind your ear where the coinciding harmonic frequencies for the octave are, which is where the beats occur. This procedure is much like focusing a camera: you can sometimes tell if a picture is in focus only if you un-focus the lens first, then bring it back into sharp focus. Once you have some experience listening to the beats, tune c^l pure to form a beatless octave with c. The two notes become one, with a definite purity to the sound.

Now try the fifth c–g. The location of the coinciding harmonic frequencies for the fifth is one octave above the top note, which in this instance is g^l. Play the note g^l several times to get its pitch "in your ear" and then play the interval c–g. The tuning tool should be on the g tuning pin. Lower and raise the pitch of g to practice hearing the beats and manipulating the beat rate, then tune the fifth pure.

Once you have practiced tuning pure fifths, then practice setting tempered fifths according to beat rates. Most of the time, fifths will be tempered narrower than pure. When tempering a fifth, you should first tune it pure and then change one or the other note to temper it to the given beat rate. For this exercise, which uses the fifth c–g, the g will be lowered in pitch to temper the interval. If you are tempering any interval narrower than pure, you either lower the upper note or raise the lower note depending on the requirements of the temperament. This is explained in chapter 6.

Once c–g is tuned pure, use a watch with an intermittent second hand—one that jumps ahead every second rather than a "sweep" second hand—and first get a sense of the seconds ticking by. Place the watch on the wrist of the hand that plays the notes so it is easily in view, or place the watch on the instrument in a convenient spot (for example, on the wrestplank with a soft cloth underneath it). Play the interval every four seconds, making the depression of the keys coincide with the "tick" of the second hand. As the four seconds go by—one, two, three, four—do the following: *play, listen, listen, listen.* You are listening rhythmically as the seconds tick by, and on the three "listening seconds" you are counting the beats. Once you can hear the beats and can count the number of beats per second, practice setting the fifth interval narrower than pure 2 beats per second. Beat rates slower than this may be difficult to hear; 2 beats per second is possible with some practice, but 1 beat per second is sometimes difficult to hear. If you have trouble determining 1 beat per second, get a sense of where the pure interval is, turn the tuning tool to get 2 beats per second, and then just find a spot in between. Another way to do this is to tune the interval pure, then narrow it just so there is a slight, pleasant, non-pure waviness in the sound—the chorus effect—without readily discernible beats. You could also switch to the same interval an octave higher, where the beat rate would be twice as fast and possibly easier to hear.

When the fifth interval c–g is mastered, move on to the fourth c–f and the major third c–e. For each interval, identify the pitch location where the beats occur (table 5.1), practice setting the pure intervals, then practice setting the tempered intervals: 1 to 2 beats per second wider than pure for the fourths, 2 to 5 beats per second wider than pure for the major thirds. For this exercise, e or f is raised in pitch to temper c–e or c–f wider than pure. If you are tempering any interval wider than pure, you either raise the upper note or lower the lower note depending on the requirements of the temperament. Again, this is explained in chapter 6.

Once you are used to hearing the beats for the different intervals, practice tempering fifths, fourths, and major thirds using root tones other than c in the tenor octave. Finally, practice setting pure and wide major sixths, particularly c–a in the range of 2 to 6 beats per second. Pure and narrow minor thirds may also be attempted, but these are rarely used.

As an alternative to counting the number of beats per second with a watch, you can use words with a certain number of syllables with which to compare beats. That is, if you develop a sense of the spacing of seconds as they tick by, words such as those in table 5.2 may be used as guides to setting beat rates. Each word is repeated in such a way that it "fills up" the time of one second. Then the beat rate of the interval to be tempered is adjusted to match the "syllable rate" of the word.[2]

Table 5.2. Words for Setting Beat Rates

Bps[a]	Word	Bps[a]	Word
2	double	5	university
3	triangle	6	indistinguishable
4	variation	7	individuality

a. Beats per second

Some people suggest the use of a metronome,[3] which may be used in two respects. First, when it is set to a speed of 60, the clicks are one second apart, which offers a reference for setting a certain number of beats per second by ear. That is, it is merely an alternative to the second hand on a watch. (The shorthand representation of this metronome setting is M.M. = 60, where "M.M." stands for "Maelzel Metronome" after the person who did not invent it but whose name is often associated with it.) Second, the metronome may be set to a given speed which corresponds to a particular beat rate. For this, the conversion factor is 60; 1 beat per second corresponds to a metronome setting of 60 (1 × 60 = 60), 2 beats per second corresponds to M.M. = 120 (2 × 60 = 120), 1.7 beats per second to M.M. = 102, and so on. For beat rates that produce settings beyond the capacity of the metronome—for example, 5 beats per second is M.M. = 300—multiply the beat rate by 15, which is one-quarter of 60. The resulting metronome speed then produces one click for every four beats in the beat rate. For example, 5 beats per second times 15 gives M.M. = 75. If you set an interval to beat four times for every click at M.M. = 75, the interval will be set at 5 beats per second. For fractional beat rates such as 5.2 beats per second, this corresponds to a metronome setting of 5.2 × 15 = 78; setting an interval to beat four times per click at M.M. = 78 yields 5.2 beats per second.

Mechanical metronomes are too loud and will interfere with your perception of beats. To avoid this, start the metronome at a given setting and get that beat rate "in your head." Then turn off the metronome and temper the interval to that rate. Alternately, an electronic metronome with a visual readout might be useful as a silent reference.

Equal-Beating Intervals

Some of the tuning instructions in chapter 6 have equal-beating intervals, so setting two intervals to the same beat rate should also be practiced. In some respects this is easier than setting a single interval to a specific beat rate, especially when the beat rate is very slow or is a fractional number.

Tune *c* and *d* roughly to pitch, tune *g* pure to *c*, and tune *a* pure to *d*. Now lower *g* so that *c–g* is tempered slightly narrower than pure, about 1 to 2 beats per second. Now place the tuning tool on the tuning pin for the *a* string, and play the intervals *c–g* and *d–a* alternately; the change from one interval to the other should be about once or twice per second. Lower the pitch of *a*, and listen to the sound of the two intervals. You are not counting the number of beats per second; you are rather comparing the quality or "color" of the two intervals that their beat rates impart to them. A useful term for this is *beat character*. As you continue to lower the pitch of a, you will find the intervals soon will not have the same beat character because d–a has become narrower than c–g. Re-tune a pure to d and repeat the exercise until you can lower the pitch of a so that c–g and d–a have a similar beat character.

Repeat this exercise with the fourths d–g and e–a. Set d and e roughly to pitch, tune g pure to d, and tune a pure to e. Raise g slightly to temper d–g wider than pure, then manipulate the pitch of a while you compare the beat character of d–g and e–a. If you get disoriented, stop and re-tune e–a pure, then adjust the pitch of a again.

Tempering intervals by means of beat character is not limited to the same class of interval; that is, one can set the fourth d–g equal-beating to the major third f–a or set the major sixth d–b equal-beating to the major third d–$f\sharp$.

Wide or Narrow?

When tempering an interval, it is important to understand that, whether the interval is narrower than pure at 2 beats per second or wider than pure at 2 beats per second, you will be unable to tell by the number of beats whether it is wide or narrow. In other words, 2 beats wide sounds the same as 2 beats narrow. It is good practice to initially tune a to-be-tempered interval pure, then widen or narrow it from that reference point. Again, always be aware of "where" the pure interval is, and also be aware when you are raising or lowering the pitch of a particular string whether you are narrowing or widening the interval.

When following tuning instructions in which two intervals are said to "beat at the same rate," it is not necessarily true that they are both wider than pure or both narrower than pure; one could be wide and the other could be narrow.

The C–G–D–A–E Complex

One important characteristic of many of the temperaments discussed here is the tempering of the fifths C–G, G–D, D–A, and A–E, which will be referred to as the C–G–D–A–E complex. These four fifths often have the same tempering in any given temperament, as shown in table 5.3. The beat rates of the intervals c–a and c–e are included to illustrate

Table 5.3. Tempering of the C–G–D–A–E Complex

Temperament	Tempering	c–a Beat Rate	c–e Beat Rate
1/4-comma meantone, Kirnberger III, and Rameau	–1/4 SC	+2.0	0
ordinaire and Kellner	–1/5 PC	+2.8	+1.0
Vallotti, Young 2, Neidhardt, Young 1, Barnes, and Lindley	–1/6 PC	+3.7	+2.2
1/6-comma meantone	–1/6 SC	+4.1	+2.7
equal	–1/12 PC	+5.9	+5.2

a useful tempering technique. In terms of the interval c–a, once either a or c is tuned to the appropriate pitch, the beat rate of the interval may be used to set the other note. Then, the rest of the steps for laying the bearings would be the same. This allows the same set of instructions to be used from either an a or c starting note. It is convenient that the beat rates for the c–a interval are in the range of beats that are easy to hear, approximately 2 to 6 beats per second. Once c and a are set in this manner, this allows you to set the notes g and d to "fit inside" c and a; that is, to temper c–g and d–a narrower than pure to have the same beat character. (As mentioned in chapter 4 with respect to equal-size versus equal-beating intervals, d–a has a slightly higher beat rate than c–g when they are tempered by the same amount, but to temper them to the same beat rate is easier and not too far from theoretical, since the difference in the beat rates of these particular fifths is only a few tenths of a beat.) In terms of the actual tuning process, with c and a set, one alternates between the d and g tuning pins, constantly adjusting the pitch of both strings, listening to the beat rate of each in relation to the other, until the two fifths have the same beat character.

The interval c–e may also be set as a guidepost. Once c–e is set, one can adjust d, g, and a to "fit inside" c–e; that is, temper c–g and d–a narrower than pure to have the same beat character, and temper d–g and e–a wider than pure to have the same beat character.

This tempering technique will be encountered with many tuning instructions, so a strong familiarity with it is worthwhile.

The Tuning Process

General Principles

The first step in the tuning process is to set either a or c to a tuning fork using the technique suggested above. In the instructions in chapter 6, you will notice a phrase such as "tune **a** to pitch," meaning the A below middle C. You should understand that an A440 tuning fork gives a tone at a^l, an octave above a. Most people do not find it difficult to tune a from an a^l fork, but if you want to, tune a^l on the instrument first, then tune a pure to a^l. Likewise, the phrase "tune **c** to pitch" refers to tenor C, which is two octaves below a C523.3 tuning fork.

Now the other eleven notes in the chromatic scale are set according to the requirements of the selected temperament; that is, one lays the bearings. The instructions for this are given in chapter 6.

Once the bearings are set, the remaining strings in the instrument are tuned by means of pure octaves. Assuming one lays the bearings in the tenor octave, next tune the notes bass-ward to this: B pure to b, $B\flat$ pure to $b\flat$, A pure to a, and so on, down to the last string. Next tune the strings treble-ward to the tenor octave: c^l pure to c, $c\sharp^l$ pure to $c\sharp$, d^l pure to d, and so on, all the way to the top. This is only one approach, but it is the most straightforward. Some people lay the bearings in the tenor octave and immediately tune the next higher octave so they can assess the tempering by playing chords. Some people tune treble-ward first then bass-ward.

Considerations for the Harpsichord

Select a register to begin the tuning process. For a harpsichord with only one eight-foot register, there is no choice. For an instrument with two eight-foot registers, you have a choice: either the front eight-foot register ("front eight"), which is the set of strings plucked by the row of jacks closest to the player, or the back eight-foot register ("back eight"), which is the set of strings plucked by the row of jacks farther from the player. Note that these terms refer to the jacks, *not* the tuning pins; in most instruments, the "front eight"—the closer jacks—have their tuning pins farther from the player. Many people suggest beginning with the front eight-foot register. This set of strings is plucked closer to the nut, which means there are more upper harmonic frequencies in the sound, and it is supposedly easier to hear the beats. On the other hand, any plucked string is rich in upper harmonic frequencies, and many people find no problem with the back eight. My suggestion is to use whichever rank of strings lets you hear beats the best. If either register works for you, then you have a choice.

Once the first register is completed, engage the second eight-foot register (if present), and tune the second register to the first by pure unisons. Start at c^1, and tune all the unisons bass-ward to this point; then return to c^1, and tune all the unisons treble-ward. Make sure that when you switch to tuning the back eight-foot register that you are really tuning the back eight-foot register; that is, make sure you are on the correct set of tuning pins. Do not make the mistake of tuning the already-tuned front eight-foot register to the un-tuned back eight-foot register

If a four-foot register is present, tune this last, using only the original front eight-foot register, with the back eight-foot register disengaged. The four-foot register may be tuned from c^1 bass-ward then from $c\sharp^1$ treble-ward, or simply from lowest note to highest note.

Some builders advocate alternate sequences for tuning octaves and unisons in an effort to distribute the tension in the strings evenly, which may help to provide a more stable long-term tuning. For example:

1. lay the bearings, front eight;
2. tune the front eight from the bearing octave bass-ward by octaves;
3. tune the back eight to the front eight by unisons from the lowest
   string to the bearing octave inclusive;
4. tune the front eight from the bearing octave treble-ward by octaves;
5. tune the back eight to the front eight by unisons from the bearing
   octave treble-ward;
6. tune the four-foot to the front eight from bass to treble.

This method requires careful attention, since one is jumping among different rows of tuning pins.

Be mindful if the instrument has a transposing keyboard and a staggered tuning pin arrangement—that is, the tuning pins for the sharps are offset from the naturals as the keyboard arrangement itself. The staggered arrangement corresponds to only one keyboard position.

Considerations for the Clavichord

The special requirement for the clavichord is that you need to use similar pressure on the keys while tuning, because variations in pressure will cause slight variations in pitch. The bass strings require particular attention, because sometimes they need to be attacked more forcefully to be heard, and this needs to be taken into account during the tuning process.

Concerning the stringing of clavichords, there are two different aspects that need to be kept in mind. The first is the number of strings per key. If the clavichord has only one string per key, the tuning process is the same as for a harpsichord. If there are two or three strings per key—that is, multiple unisons, what is called double or triple stringing—the tuning process is different. Since these multiple unisons are not capable of being turned on and off as with harpsichord registers, small rubber wedges must be used to mute the strings that are not being tuned. The second aspect is that some clavichords are made with fewer sets of unison strings than keys. This is referred to as fretting. A double-fretted clavichord would have, for example, the notes c^1 and $c\#^1$ being played from the same set of unison strings (whether one, two, or three strings). A triple-fretted clavichord would have, for example, the notes b, c^1, and $c\#^1$ played from the same set of unison strings. Double- and triple-fretted clavichords have their temperaments built into them, because the tangents at the end of the keys are in predetermined positions. Thus, laying the bearings for fretted clavichords is easier.

Clavichords typically have their tuning pins at the extreme right of the case, roughly parallel to the case side. This means that you need to pay particular attention to which tuning pin you are on, especially when there are multiple unisons.

Considerations for the Fortepiano

Fortepianos also have multiple unisons, requiring that one use wedges or felt as one lays the bearings and then tunes up and down by octaves. The keys are often struck very hard as the instrument is tuned to be sure the pitch is "set," since the performer has the capability of playing *fortissimo*.

Electronic Tuners

These devices serve as an aid to tuning notes. It is the opinion of this author that tuning and tempering by ear by means of a tuning fork is an important skill to acquire. It should also be appreciated that the human ear and an electronic tuner do not "hear" things in the same manner, and in some respects the ear is superior.[4] However, there are certain circumstances in which an electronic tuner may be useful: when one is setting a complicated temperament; when a particularly precise tuning is needed for a concert or a multi-session recording; or when there is too much ambient noise.[5] A particularly useful mode for an electronic tuner is to allow one to lay the bearings if the cent deviations from equal temperament are known; these are given in chapter 12. If the electronic tuner is able to sound a reference tone, this may also be useful as a substitute for a tuning fork.

Summary

The tuning process with respect to the stringed keyboard instruments refers to all the steps involved in adjusting all the strings to their proper pitches. It involves (1) setting a reference string to pitch; (2) laying the bearings, or tuning and tempering the remaining eleven notes of the chromatic scale at or near the tenor octave according to the temperament; and (3) tuning all other strings by pure octaves to the bearing octave or by unisons between registers.

The tools needed are one or more tuning forks and a tuning tool. The use of the tuning fork involves activating the tuning fork while tuning the reference string to pitch. The use of the tuning tool involves identifying the correct tuning pin, proper placement and removal, correct movement for control of pin rotation, and minimal movement.

Listening for beats is a skill that needs to be practiced. One should ultimately be able to set: pure unisons, octaves, fifths, fourths, and major thirds; fifths narrower than pure from 1 to 2 beats per second; fourths wider than pure from 1 to 2 beats per second; major thirds wider than pure from 2 to 5 beats per second; and major sixths wider than pure 2 to 6 beats per second. Once these are mastered, one should have no problem with the occasional narrow minor third or wide fifth. References for seconds-ticking-by include the second hand on a wrist watch, or a metronome; references for judging beat rates include a metronome or the syllable rate of selected words. One should be able to set two intervals to beat equally by virtue of their beat character.

One must always be attentive to where the pure interval is and whether an interval is being tempered wider or narrower than pure.

The C–G–D–A–E complex is a recurring pattern in many temperaments, so a familiarity with the way fifths and fourths are tempered within this complex is useful.

Electronic tuners have their uses, but they are generally no substitute for the skill of tuning and tempering by ear.

Notes

1. Ann Bond, *A Guide to the Harpsichord* (Portland, Oreg.: Amadeus Press, 1997), 234–43; Claudio Di Veroli, *Unequal Temperaments and Their Role in the Performance of Early Music* (Buenos Aires: Artes Gráficas Farro, 1978), 157–68; Frank Hubbard, *Harpsichord Regulating and Repairing* (Boston: Tuners Supply, 1963), 29–32; Owen Jorgensen, *The Equal-Beating Temperaments*, 2nd ed. (Hendersonville, N.C.: Sunbury Press, 2000), 9–12; G. C. Klop, *Harpsichord Tuning*, trans. Glen Wilson (Garderen, Holland: Werkplaats voor Clavecimbelbouw, 1974. Reprint 1983), 1–8; Edward L. Kottick, *The Harpsichord Owner's Guide: A Manual for Buyers and Owners* (Chapel Hill: University of North Carolina Press, 1987), 149–63; Howard Schott, *Playing the Harpsichord* (New York: St. Martin's Press, 1979), 208–14; Martin B. Tittle, *A Performer's Guide through Historical Keyboard Tunings*, rev. ed. (Ann Arbor, Mich.: Anderson Press, 1987), 16–37; and Richard Troeger, *Technique and Interpretation on the Harpsichord and Clavichord* (Bloomington: Indiana University Press, 1987), 205–17.

2. Brian Worsfold, "English Prosody: Word Stress Databases," n.d., http://www.udl.es/usuaris/m0163949/englpros.htm (21 October 2004).

3. Klop, *Harpsichord Tuning*, 6; and Tittle, *A Performer's Guide*, 29.

4. Paul Poletti, "Temperaments for Dummies," 2001/2003, http://www.polettipiano.com/Media/T4D.PDF (9 September 2003).

5. Poletti, "Temperaments for Dummies."

6

Instructions for Setting
Selected Temperaments

The following instructions present the list of intervals that need to be tuned and tempered in order to lay the bearings for the temperaments described in chapter 2.

The note in bold type is the one that is adjusted. The direction the note is tuned—either up to raise the pitch or down to lower the pitch—may be understood in the following ways:

If the instructions read:	*do the following:*
temper c–**e** wider than pure	raise the note e
temper **c**–e wider than pure	lower the note c
temper c–**g** narrower than pure	lower the note g
temper **c**–g narrower than pure	raise the note c

The convention of denoting pitches by italics is suspended for the tuning instructions in the interest of maximum clarity. In addition to the written instructions such as "temper **e**–a wider than pure, 2 beats per second," the calculated beat rates are given in parentheses for completeness. With respect to the beat rates, "+2.1" signifies an interval wider than pure at 2.1 beats per second; "–1.2" signifies an interval narrower than pure at 1.2 beats per second. The fact that the values are given to one-tenth of a beat does not mean the interval needs to be set that precisely. The beat rates are based on an A440 pitch reference; other pitch references are discussed at the end of the chapter. Following the instructions for each temperament, the range of notes set while laying the bearings is given. Notice that some instructions have notes that are skipped over and which would need to be filled in when tuning by octaves.

97

Alternate instructions for setting these and other temperaments are available from additional sources.[1]

If one enumerates the tempering steps in the following instructions, one can get a sense of the level of difficulty in laying the bearings for each temperament (table 6.1). The number of tempering steps refers to those intervals that must be tempered wider or narrower than pure; it excludes pure intervals and the initial note tuned to the tuning fork.

Table 6.1. Number of Tempering Steps for Selected Temperaments

Name	No.	Name	No.
Pythagorean tuning	0	Barnes	5
1/4-comma meantone	3	Lindley	6
Werckmeister III	3	Neidhardt	7
Kirnberger III	3	*tempérament ordinaire*	7
Rameau	4	Sorge	7
Kellner	4	Young no. 1	7
Vallotti	5	1/6-comma meantone	11
Young no. 2	5	equal temperament	11

Pythagorean Tuning
from a
tune **a** to pitch
tune pure: **e**–a, e–**b**, f♯–b, c♯–f♯, c♯–g♯
tune pure: **d**–a, d–g, c–g, c–f, f–b♭, e♭–b♭
from c
tune **c** to pitch
tune pure: c–**g**, **d**–g, d–**a**, **e**–a, e–**b**, f♯–b, c♯–f♯, c♯–g♯
tune pure: c–**f**, f–b♭, e♭–b♭
range: c to b

1/4-Comma Meantone Temperament

tune **a** or **c** to pitch

temper **c**–a or c–**a** (depending on the starting note) wider than pure,
    2 beats per second (+2.0)

tune pure: c–**e**

check: e–a beats as c–a (+2.0)

temper c–**g** narrower than pure, 1 beat per second (–1.2)

temper **d**–a narrower than pure, to beat similar to c–g (–1.4 vs. –1.2)

check: d–g beats similar to e–a (+1.8 vs. +2.0)

tune pure: d–**d**^{1}, **f**–a, g–**b**, e$\flat$–g, d–**f**$\sharp$, e–**g**$\sharp$, **b**$\flat$–d^1, a–**c**$\sharp^1$

range: c, d to b, c$\sharp^1$, d^1

optional: to obtain a D$\sharp$ instead of an E$\flat$, tune pure: **B**–b, B–**d**$\sharp$

optional: to obtain an A$\flat$ instead of a G$\sharp$, tune pure: c–**c**^{1}, **a**$\flat$–c^1

Werckmeister III

from a

tune **a** to pitch

temper **f**–a wider than pure, 2 beats per second (+2.0)

tune pure: **c**–f

(go to *)

from c

tune **c** to pitch

tune pure: c–**f**

temper f–**a** wider than pure, 2 beats per second (+2.0)

*check: c–a beats less than f–a (+1.5 vs. +2.0)

tune pure: **e**–a, e–**b**

check: c–e beats as c–a (+1.5)

tune pure: f–**b**$\flat$, e$\flat$–b$\flat$, e$\flat$–**g**$\sharp$, **c**$\sharp$–g$\sharp$, c$\sharp$–**f**$\sharp$

temper **d**–a narrower than pure to beat as c–e and c–a
    (–1.5 vs. +1.5 vs. +1.5)

temper d–**g** wider than pure, 2 beats per second (+2.0)

check: d–g beats as f–a (+2.0)

check: c–g beats almost as d–a (–1.3 vs. –1.5)

range: c to b

Kirnberger III
tune **a** or **c** to pitch
temper **c**–a or c–**a** (depending on the starting note) wider than pure,
    2 beats per second (+2.0)
tune pure: c–**e**
check: e–a beats as c–a (+2.0)
temper c–**g** narrower than pure, 1 beat per second (−1.2)
temper **d**–a narrower than pure, to beat similar to c–g (−1.4 vs. −1.2)
check: d–g beats similar to e–a (+1.8 vs. +2.0)
tune pure: c–**f**, f–**b**♭, e♭–b♭, e♭ –**g**♯, **c**♯–g♯, e–**b**, **f**♯–b
range: c to b

Vallotti
from a
tune **a** to pitch
temper **f**–a wider than pure, 3 beats per second (+3.0)
temper f–**c**^{1} slightly narrower than pure (−1.2)
tune pure: **c**–c^1
(go to *)
from c
tune **c** to pitch
tune pure: c–**c**^{1}
temper **f**–c^1 slightly narrower than pure (−1.2)
temper f–**a** wider than pure, 3 beats per second (+3.0)
*check: c–a is wider than pure, almost 4 beats per second (+3.7)
tune pure: f–**b**♭, e♭–b♭, e♭–**g**♯, **c**♯–g♯, c♯–**f**♯
temper **d**–f♯ wider than pure, 4 beats per second (+4.2)
temper c–**e** wider than pure, 2 beats per second (+2.2)
check: e–a is wider than pure, less than 2 beats per second (+1.5)
temper c–**g** narrower than pure, to beat similar to d–a (−0.9 vs. −1.0)
tune pure: f♯–**b**
range: c to c^1

Young No. 2
tune **c** to pitch
tune pure: c–**c**^{1}, c–**f**, f–**b**♭, e♭–b♭, e♭–g♯, c♯–g♯, c♯–f♯
temper c–**e** wider than pure, 2 beats per second (+2.2)
temper **d**–f♯ wider than pure, between 2 and 3 beats per second (+2.5)
temper d–**b** wider than pure, 4 beats per second (+4.2)
temper **g**–c^1 wider than pure, to beat similar to f♯–b (+1.8 vs. +1.7)
check: g–b is wider than pure, 3 beats per second (+3.3)
check: c–g beats similar to e–b (–0.9 vs. –1.1)
temper d–**a** narrower than pure, to beat as c–g (–1.0 vs. –0.9)
range: c to c^1

Neidhardt Circulating Temperament No. 1
from a
tune **a** to pitch
temper **f**–a wider than pure, 5 beats per second (+5.0)
tune pure: **c**–f, f–**b**♭
(go to *)
from c
tune **c** to pitch
tune pure: c–**f**, f–**b**♭
temper f–**a** wider than pure, 5 beats per second (+5.0)
*check: c–a is wider than pure, almost 4 beats per second (+3.7)
temper c–**e** wider than pure, 2 beats per second (+2.2)
temper c–**g** narrower than pure, 1 beat per second (–0.9)
temper **d**–a narrower than pure, to beat similar to c–g (–1.0 vs. –0.9)
check: d–g beats similar to e–a (+1.3 vs. +1.5)
temper d–**b** wider than pure, 5 beats per second (+5.0)
check: d–b beats as f–a (+5.0)
check: g–b is wider than pure, 4 beats per second (+4.4)
check: e–b is very nearly pure (–0.6)
temper d–**f♯** wider than pure, 4 beats per second (+4.2)
tune pure: **c♯**–f♯, c♯–**g♯**
temper **e**♭–b♭ to beat similar to e–b (–0.5 vs. –0.6)
check: c♯–f beats as e♭–g (+7.1)
range: c to b

Tempérament Ordinaire
tune **a** or **c** to pitch
temper **c**–a or c–**a** (depending on the starting note) wider than pure,
    3 beats per second (+2.8)
tune pure: c–**c**^{1}
temper **g**–c^1 wider than pure, 2 beats per second (+2.1)
temper **e**–a wider than pure, 2 beats per second (+1.8)
temper **d**–g wider than pure, to beat similar to e–a (+1.6 vs. +1.8)
temper d–**f♯** wider than pure, 3 beats per second (+3.2)
tune pure: f♯–**b**, c♯–**f♯**, c♯–**g♯**, e♭–**g♯**
check: d–b beats as d–f♯ (+3.2)
temper **f**–c^1 narrower than pure, to beat similar to e–b (−1.4 vs. −1.3)
temper f–**b**♭ *narrower* than pure, to beat similar to c–g (−1.0 vs. −1.1)
check: e♭–b♭ is slightly *wider* than pure
range: c to c^1

1/6-Comma Meantone Temperament
tune **a** or **c** to pitch
temper **c**–a or c–**a** (depending on the starting note) wider than pure,
    4 beats per second (+4.1)
temper c–**e** wider than pure, 3 beats per second (+2.7)
temper c–**e**♭ narrower than pure, 5 beats per second (−4.9)
temper e♭–**g** wider than pure, 3 beats per second (+3.2)
temper g–**b** wider than pure, 4 beats per second, to beat as c–a (+4.1)
temper e♭–**b**♭ narrower than pure, to beat as e–b (−1.0)
temper **d**–a narrower than pure, to beat similar to c–g (−0.9 vs. −0.8)
temper d–**f♯** wider than pure, 3 beats per second, to beat similar to
    e♭–g (+3.0 vs. +3.2)
temper **f**–b♭ wider than pure, to beat as f♯–b (+1.5)
temper **c♯**–f♯ wider than pure, to beat as c–f (+1.1)
temper c♯–**g♯** narrower than pure, to beat as d–a (−0.9)
range: c to b

Rameau
tune **a** or **c** to pitch
temper **c**–a or c–**a** (depending on the starting note) wider than pure,
    2 beats per second (+2.0)
tune pure: c–**e**, **f**–a
check: e–a beats as c–a (+2.0)
temper c–**g** narrower than pure, slightly more than 1 beat per second
    (–1.2)
temper **d**–a narrower than pure, to beat as c–g (–1.4 vs. –1.2)
check: d–g beats similar to e–a (+1.8 vs. +2.0)
tune pure: **B**♭–d, B♭–**b**♭, g–**b**, **f**♯–b, **c**♯–f♯, c♯–**g**♯
check: d–f♯ beats as f–b♭ and d–b (+2.3 vs. +2.2 vs. +2.3)
temper **e**♭–b♭ *wider* than pure, 2 beats per second (+1.9)
check: e♭–g♯ is *narrower* than pure, and beats similar to d–f
    (–2.6 vs. –2.7)
range: c to b, plus B♭

Sorge
from a
tune **a** to pitch
temper **f**–a wider than pure, 5 beats per second (+5.0)
tune pure: **c**–f
(go to *)
from c
tune **c** to pitch
tune pure: c–**f**
temper f–**a** wider than pure, 5 beats per second (+5.0)
*check: c–a is wider than pure, almost 4 beats per second (+3.7)
tune pure: **e**–a
check: c–e beats as c–a (+3.7)
temper a–**d**¹ wider than pure, 2 beats per second (+2.0)
tune pure: **d**–d¹
temper d–**f**♯ wider than pure, 5 beats per second (+5.0)
temper c–**g** narrower than pure, to beat as d–a (–0.9 vs. –1.0)
temper e–**b** narrower than pure, to beat as d–a (–1.1 vs. –1.0)
temper f–**b**♭ wider than pure, to beat as f♯–b (+0.8)
tune **e**♭–b♭ slightly narrower than pure (–0.5) or tune pure
tune pure: e♭–**g**♯, **c**♯–g♯
range: c to b, plus d¹

Young No. 1
tune **a** to pitch
temper a–$\mathbf{d}^1$ wider than pure, 2 beats per second (+2.0)
tune pure: $\mathbf{d}$–d^1
temper **f**–a wider than pure, 4 beats per second (+4.0)
temper d–**f**♯ wider than pure, 4 beats per second, to beat similar to f–a
    (+4.2 vs. +4.0)
tune pure: **c**♯–f♯, c♯–**g**♯, e♭–g♯, e♭–**b**♭
temper f♯–**b** wider than pure to beat as f–b♭ (+0.8)
temper **g**–b wider than pure to beat similar to f–a (+4.4 vs. +4.0)
temper **c**–g narrower than pure to beat similar to d–a (–0.9 vs. –1.0)
tune pure: c–$\mathbf{c}^1$
temper **e**–b narrower than pure to beat as f–c^1 (–0.6)
check: c–e is wider than pure, 2 beats per second (+2.2)
range: c to c^1, plus d^1

Kellner
tune **a** or **c** to pitch
temper **c**–a or c–**a** (depending on the starting note) wider than pure,
    less than 3 beats per second (+2.8)
tune pure: c–$\mathbf{c}^1$, c–**f**, f–**b**♭, e♭–b♭, e♭–**g**♯, c♯–g♯, c♯–**f**♯
temper f♯–**b** wider than pure, 2 beats per second (+2.0)
tune pure: **e**–b
temper **g**–c^1 wider than pure, to beat similar to f♯–b (+2.1 vs. +2.0)
temper **d**–a narrower than pure, to beat similar to c–g (–1.2 vs. –1.1)
range: c to c^1

Barnes
from a
tune **a** to pitch
temper **f**–a wider than pure, 3 beats per second (+3.0)
temper f–$\mathbf{c}^1$ slightly narrower than pure (–1.2)
tune pure: $\mathbf{c}$–c^1
(go to *)
from c
tune **c** to pitch
tune pure: c–$\mathbf{c}^1$
temper **f**–c^1 slightly narrower than pure (–1.2)
temper f–**a** wider than pure, 3 beats per second (+3.0)

*check: c–a is wider than pure, almost 4 beats per second (+3.7)
tune pure: f–b♭, e♭–b♭, e♭–g♯, c♯–g♯, c♯–f♯
temper **d**–f♯ wider than pure, 4 beats per second (+4.2)
temper c–**e** wider than pure, 2 beats per second (+2.2)
check: e–a is wider than pure, less than 2 beats per second (+1.5)
temper c–**g** narrower than pure, to beat similar to d–a (–0.9 vs. –1.0)
tune pure: e–**b**
range: c to c¹

(Note that the instructions for Barnes are the same as those for Vallotti, except for the last step: b is tuned pure to f♯ in Vallotti, while b is tuned pure to e in Barnes.[2])

Lindley
tune **a** to pitch
temper **f**–a wider than pure, 4 beats per second (+4.0)
tune pure: f–b♭, e♭–b♭, e♭–g♯, c♯–g♯, c♯–f♯
temper **d**–f♯ wider than pure, 3 beats per second (+3.3)
temper d–**b** wider than pure, 4 beats per second (+4.2)
check: d–a beats similar to f♯–b (–1.0 vs. +0.8)
temper **g**–b wider than pure, 3 beats per second, to beat as d–f♯ (+3.3)
temper **e**–b narrower than pure, to beat similar to d–a (–1.1 vs. –1.0)
temper **c**–g narrower than pure, to beat similar to d–a (–0.9 vs. –1.0)
range: c to b

Equal Temperament
To set equal temperament by ear requires considerable practice. It is suggested that one explore the alternatives first: either use an electronic tuner to set the twelve notes, or use the instructions for the easier near-equal temperament in chapter 10.
tune **c**¹ to pitch
tune pure: **c**–c¹
temper c–**e** wider than pure (+5.2)
temper e–**g**♯ wider than pure (+6.5)
check: g♯–c¹ beats slightly more than 8 beats per second (+8.2)
adjust **g**, **d**, and **a** to "fit inside" c–e; for example:
    temper c–**g** narrower than pure (–0.4)
    temper **d**–g wider than pure (+0.7)
    temper d–**a** narrower than pure (–0.5)

adjust **b**, **f**♯, and **c**♯^{1} to "fit inside" e–g♯; for example:
    temper e–**b** narrower than pure (–0.6)
    temper **f**♯–b wider than pure (+0.8)
    temper f♯–**c**♯^{1} narrower than pure (–0.6)
tune pure: **c**♯–c♯^{1}
check: c♯–g♯ is narrower than pure (–0.5)
adjust **e**♭, **b**♭, and **f** to "fit inside" g♯–c^1; for example:
    temper **e**♭–g♯ wider than pure (+0.7)
    temper e♭–**b**♭ narrower than pure (–0.5)
    temper **f**–b♭ wider than pure (+0.8)
check: c♯–f beats at +5.5
check: the thirds c–e, d–f♯, e–g♯, f♯–b♭, and g♯–c^1 should beat
    progressively faster (+5.2, +5.8, +6.5, +7.3, +8.2)
range: c to c♯^{1}

Beat Rates at Other Pitch References

The beat rates given in the above instructions were calculated at an A440 pitch reference. In table 6.2, A440 beat rates in increments of one-half beat per second are converted to beat rates at three other pitch references: A466, A415, and A392. For all practical purposes, the change of one semitone is negligible; that is, one can use the beat rates given in the above instructions at an A466 or an A415 pitch. The two-semitone difference between A440 and A392 may introduce some discrepancies, especially at the higher beat rates. If A392 is the pitch reference of choice, allowances might need to be made, even to the point of generating a unique set of tuning instructions based on a specific set of A392 beat rates (see chapter 4).

Table 6.2. Beat Rates at Different Pitch References, in Beats Per Second

A466	A440	A415	A392
0.5	0.5	0.5	0.4
1.1	1.0	0.9	0.9
1.6	1.5	1.4	1.3
2.1	2.0	1.9	1.8
2.6	2.5	2.4	2.2
3.2	3.0	2.8	2.7
3.7	3.5	3.3	3.1
4.2	4.0	3.8	3.6
4.8	4.5	4.2	4.0
5.3	5.0	4.7	4.5
5.8	5.5	5.2	4.9
6.4	6.0	5.7	5.3
6.9	6.5	6.1	5.8
7.4	7.0	6.6	6.2
7.9	7.5	7.1	6.7
8.5	8.0	7.6	7.1

Notes

1. Carey Beebe, "Resources: Technical Library: Tuning, Temperament," 2003, http://www.hpschd.nu (12 July 2003); William Blood, "'Well-Tempering' the Clavier: Five Methods," *Early Music* 7 (October 1979): 491, 493, 495; Dale C. Carr, "A Practical Introduction to Unequal Temperament," *Diapason* 65 (February 1974): 6–8; Claudio Di Veroli, *Unequal Temperaments and Their Role in the Performance of Early Music* (Buenos Aires: Artes Gráficas Farro, 1978), 169–98; Owen Jorgensen, *The Equal-Beating Temperaments*, 2nd ed. (Hendersonville, N.C.: Sunbury Press, 2000); Owen Jorgensen, *Tuning: Containing the Perfection of Eighteenth-Century Temperament, the Lost Art of Nineteenth-Century Temperament, and the Science of Equal Temperament, Complete with Instructions for Aural and Electronic Tuning* (East Lansing: Michigan State University Press, 1991); Owen Jorgensen, *Tuning the Historical Temperaments by Ear* (Marquette: Northern Michigan University Press, 1977); Herbert A. Kellner, *The Tuning of My Harpsichord* (Frankfurt/Main: Verlag Das Musikinstrument, 1980); Mark Lindley, "Instructions for the Clavier Diversely Tempered," *Early Music* 5 (January 1977): 18–23; Mark Lind-

ley, "Tuning Renaissance and Baroque Keyboard Instruments: Some Guide-lines," *Performance Practice Review* 7 (Spring 1994): 85–92; and Phil Sloffer, "Harpsichord Tuning and Repair," n.d., http://music.indiana.edu/som/piano_repair/temperaments/ (14 July 2003).
      2. Bradley Lehman, personal communication, 13 April 2005.

7

A Historical Overview

This chapter presents selected historical aspects of temperament. It is intended as a general guide to the references to meantone temperaments, the well-tempered systems, and equal temperament from approximately 1500 to 1800. This outline is based on several published summaries.[1]

The chronologies are arranged separately for each category. Even though three broad categories are used, it should be remembered that there are a variety of meantone temperaments and many well-tempered systems. It should also be understood that the given years are dates of historical references which may not necessarily coincide with the time period the temperament was in actual use and may not necessarily reflect a majority opinion at that time. One must also realize that a given temperament attributed to a particular person does not exclude the possibility that the same temperament may have been discovered or discussed prior to that attribution.

The historical perspectives are intended to offer a sense of the relationship of temperament types to specific eras and composers. The references to the Renaissance period encompass the years from approximately 1450 to 1600, while the references to the Baroque era encompass the years from approximately 1600 to 1750.

In addition, two other topics are presented. One is a discussion of the many factors that need to be considered when the performer is faced with the question of which temperament to select for a particular piece of music or a particular set of circumstances. Then, a very specific instance of that question is reviewed—namely, the question of temperament and the music of J. S. Bach.

Meantone Temperaments

Selected Chronology

1482: Bartolomeo Ramos de Pareja (c1440–?1491) mentions that meantone temperament is common on keyboard instruments at that time.[2]

1523: Pietro Aaron (c1480–c1550) presents a method on how to tune meantone temperament.[3]

1558/1571: Gioseffo Zarlino (1517–1590) describes 1/4-comma meantone in precise mathematical terms[4] and calls it "very pleasing for all purposes" with respect to keyboard instruments.[5]

1618: Michael Praetorius (1571–1621) recommends only 1/4-comma meantone for keyboard instruments[6] and explains the distribution of the comma among the various intervals.[7]

1636: Marin Mersenne (1588–1648) reiterates the prominence of 1/4-comma meantone, but gives awkward tuning instructions (see below).[8]

1666: Lemme Rossi (?–1673) discusses variations of meantone temperament based on 1/5 comma and 2/9 comma, which results in major thirds slightly wider than pure.[9]

1707/1711: Joseph Sauveur (1653–1716) compares 1/4-, 1/5-, and 1/6-comma meantone, mentioning that what harpsichord and organ makers use corresponds to the 1/5-comma variety.[10]

1762: Giordano Riccati (1709–1790) presents a tuning that still has the vestige of a wolf interval.[11]

c1800: Several examples of meantone-style temperaments are still being published: in the *Encyclopedia Britannica* in 1797, by William Hawkes (dates unknown) in 1807, and by John Marsh (1752–1828) in 1809.[12]

Historical Perspectives

The approximate time span for meantone temperament is from the late fifteenth century to the early to mid-seventeenth century.[13]

The earliest keyboard composer whose use of triads as vertical sonorities seems to require meantone temperament—as opposed to a Pythagorean tuning—was Conrad Paumann (c1410–1473).[14]

Apparently no variety of meantone temperament—2/7-comma, 1/4-comma, 1/5-comma—had preferential status during the Renaissance.[15] This may be related to the fact that some of these variants are difficult to tune accurately or the fact that tuners may have been merely seeking the "spirit" of meantone: pure or near-pure major thirds and sixths, and fifths that did not beat too badly.[16]

As composers used modulations to other keys more and more by the late 1600s—well before the end of the Baroque era—this presented problems with the use of meantone temperament.[17] However, many organs were still tuned in meantone tempereament up to 1740 in north Germany[18] and up to 1850 in England.[19] This may be due to the fact that it was a long and complex task to reset an organ's temperament.

Well-Tempered Systems

Selected Chronology

1511: Arnolt Schlick (c1460–?1525) describes a temperament in which the major thirds are slightly larger than pure and the fifths are not tuned in any regular pattern as in meantone temperament.[20]

1636: Marin Mersenne (1588–1648) presents awkward tuning instructions for meantone temperament that were later misinterpreted by other authors. Interestingly enough, the result was musically useful and formed the basis for the wide fifths in *tempérament ordinaire*.[21]

1681/1691: Andreas Werckmeister (1645–1706) presents a temperament that has no wolf interval, now generally referred to as Werckmeister III.[22]

1705: Andreas Werckmeister (1645–1706) describes the changes to the organ of the Schloss-Kirche in Gröningen, near Halberstadt. Meantone temperament is mentioned as being inappropriate for the requirements of the current music.[23]

1724: Johann Georg Neidhardt (c1685–1739), an advocate of equal temperament, nevertheless acknowledges that the degree of tempering may be related to the situation; hence his famous categorization of an unequal temperament for a village, a less unequally tempered system for small and large towns, and equal temperament for a court (based on the probable use of fewer sharps and flats in a rural setting).[24]

1726: Jean-Philippe Rameau (1683–1764) praises *tempérament ordinaire*.[25]

1784: *Magazin der Musik* reports on the tuning of Muzio Clementi (1752–1832), which includes C–E beating "slightly high," E–G♯ "very high," and A♭–C "higher still."[26] This is characteristic of a well-tempered system.

Historical Perspectives

The approximate time span for well-tempered systems is from the late seventeenth century to the early nineteenth century (French *tempérament ordinaire* from the late seventeenth century, subtle German tunings in the manner of Neidhardt and Sorge from the early eighteenth century).[27]

The most characteristic keyboard tuning in the eighteenth century was a well-tempered irregular system with no wolf interval, major thirds in the key of C almost like meantone temperament, and major thirds in the keys of B or A♭ wider than equal temperament.[28]

The majority of the German Baroque temperaments that were described had the following characteristics: no major thirds wider than the Pythagorean third; fifths more heavily tempered on or near F, C, G, D, and A; and fifths that were pure or close to pure on or near E♭, G♯, C♯ and F♯.[29]

Eighteenth-century French tuning instructions had two or three fifths tuned *wider* than pure on or near G♯, E♭, and B♭; this was characteristic of *tempérament ordinaire*.[30] French Baroque unequal temperaments at the time of Jean-Philippe Rameau (1683–1764) were less subtle than German temperaments.[31]

None of the great German keyboard music of the late Baroque and Classical periods was created in an equal-temperament environment.[32]

The feature of the well-tempered systems that they have fifths of different sizes and thirds of different sizes was noted by eighteenth-century theorists and musicians as being the reason behind the concept of *key characteristics*, the assigning of a different meaning or mood to each key signature. The linking of these two topics persisted into the nineteenth century.[33]

Equal Temperament

Selected Chronology

1581: Zhu Zaiyu (Chu Tsai-yü) (1536–1611) of China presents a treatise that contains the calculations of equal-tempered semitones based on the twelfth root of two, accurate to twenty-four decimal places.[34] These calculations may have been worked out as early as 1567.[35]

1581: Vincenzo Galilei (c1520–1591), father of Galileo, describes a practical mathematical approach for determining the position of frets on lutes and viols based on the ratio 18:17, the result being a close approximation to equal-tempered semitones.[36]

c1590s: Simon Stevin (1548–1620) of Flanders is the first European to present a system of equal-tempered semitones that is based on the twelfth root of two,[37] though probably not completely independent of the work of Zhu Zaiyu.[38]

1630s: The concept of equal temperament is endorsed by Girolamo Frescobaldi (1583–1643),[39] and this endorsement is probably accepted by his student Johann Jacob Froberger (1616–1667), whose works seem suited to it.[40]

1636: Marin Mersenne (1588–1648) gives mathematical approximations of equal temperament.[41]

1702: Andreas Werckmeister (1645–1706) presents a direct argument for equal temperament.[42]

1706: Johann Georg Neidhardt (c1685–1739) describes equal temperament.[43]

1724: Johann Georg Neidhardt (c1685–1739) recommends equal temperament for a court—as opposed to a small town or village—presumably based on the greater likelihood in that setting of performing music with more sharps and flats.[44]

1737: Jean-Philippe Rameau (1683–1764) endorses equal temperament, after advocating irregular temperaments eleven years earlier.[45]

1746: Georg Andreas Sorge (1703–1778) writes that equal temperament is the best for "present musical practice," in that it makes all twenty-four key signatures usable.[46]

1756/1776: Friedrich Wilhelm Marpurg (1718–1795) advocates equal temperament, particularly for ensemble music.[47]

Historical Perspectives

The time span for equal temperament is the nineteenth and twentieth centuries, plus some sixteenth-century music.[48]

It has not been shown that Renaissance keyboard players either advocated or used equal temperament, but it appears to have been used on fretted instruments such as the lute and viol at least since the early sixteenth century.[49]

The fact that Baroque keyboard musicians resisted equal temperament may have been due to their appreciation of, or continued interest in, subtle tunings.[50]

The music of Jean-Philippe Rameau (1683–1764) is "congenial" to equal temperament.[51]

In the late seventeenth and early eighteenth centuries, many theorists became interested in equal temperament, which created a great momentum for its use; yet, most of the German organbuilders resisted until after the time of Johann Friedrich Wender (1655–1729) and Gottfried Silbermann (1683–1753).[52]

Of the leading eighteenth-century German composers, C. P. E. Bach (1714–1788) is the one whose music ought to be performed in equal temperament.[53]

Equal temperament gained acceptance in the nineteenth century. It was used in England by the Broadwood company in their pianos by the 1840s, in France by the organbuilder Aristide Cavaillé-Coll (1811–1899), and by the contemporary German organ builders.[54] There were many "near-equal" temperaments during the nineteenth century, and equal temperament set according to beat rates may be found in the early twentieth century.[55]

Comparative Chronologies

Table 7.1 lists the chronologies enumerated above in a side-by-side layout, after a format by Tittle.[56] This is not meant to be comprehensive. The entries in italics denote references to the selected temperaments presented in chapter 2. The two dashed lines delineate the Baroque era (1600–1750).

Table 7.1. Chronologies of Selected Temperament References

Meantone T.	Well-Tempered Sys.	Equal T.
1482 Ramos		
	1511 Schlick	
1523 Aaron		
1558 Zarlino		
1571 Zarlino		
		1581 Zhu
		1581 Galilei
		c1590s Stevin
1618 Praetorius		
		1630s Frescobaldi
1636 Mersenne	1636 Mersenne	1636 Mersenne
1666 Rossi		
	1681 Werckmeister	
	1691 Werckmeister	
		1702 Werckmeister
	1705 Werckmeister	
	1706 Neidhardt	
1707 Sauveur		
1711 Sauveur		
	1724 Neidhardt	1724 Neidhardt
	1726 Rameau	
	1732 Neidhardt	
		1737 Rameau
	1744 Sorge	
		1746 Sorge
	1754 Tartini (Vallotti)	
		1756 Marpurg
1762 Riccati		
	1770s Kirnberger	1776 Marpurg
	1779 Vallotti	
	1784 (Clementi)	
1797 Britannica		
	1800 Young	
1807 Hawkes		
1809 Marsh		

Temperament Selection

Di Veroli lists the following difficulties concerning the question of which temperament to use for a given piece.[57]

1. Early treatises do not discuss all musical styles in all the countries.
2. Many treatises are written by theorists who are far removed from practical experience.
3. When a temperament is described, it is unclear whether it is in common use.
4. Tuning instructions in the treatises are often ambiguous.
5. During transition periods—1480, 1620, 1750—there was no agreement about the basic questions of performance, including temperaments.
6. The opinions of some well-known musicians—especially Frescobaldi and Rameau—were strongly opposed by their contemporaries.
7. Written music does not give enough clues about the temperament for which it was written.
8. Different works by the same composer often seem to demand different temperaments; for example, Guillaume Dufay (c1400–1474), Louis Couperin (c1626–1661), and Dietrich Buxtehude (c1637–1707).

Given all these considerations, we should recognize that an exact correlation of a particular temperament with a particular piece of music may be impossible to identify.[58] However, a performer needs to be able to ascertain a range of possible temperaments for a given situation and ultimately select one. Based on the discussions by Di Veroli[59] and Troeger[60] and the material presented in this chapter and in chapter 3, the following factors need to be considered.

1. Establish in what historical period and in what country the piece was written.
2. Determine whether or not the composer had any documented views on temperament. (Very few did; Rameau is perhaps the most prominent exception.[61])
3. Review the temperament milieu at that time the piece was written, especially which theorists were writing.

4. Determine whether there was an association of the composer with any theorists. Such a connection may only be a loose one, such as simply an association of time or place.[62]

5. Examine the notation of the piece for clues, such as key signatures used and the presence of enharmonic notes.

6. Evaluate the music itself. Is the music primarily melodic or harmonic? Do chromatic passages suggest different-sized semitones? How is tension and relaxation conveyed?[63] (See chapter 3.)

7. Use your own ears to evaluate the musical impact of interval size—for example, whether wide major thirds in distant key signatures enhance or distort the musical thought.

One should also bear in mind that selection of a temperament may be seen as an interpretive decision; that is, differences in temperaments can highlight different aspects of a work, as do different performers.[64] In addition, the modern performer is often faced with the situation of presenting a concert of varied works, which requires one to select a single temperament that accommodates all the pieces.

Temperament and J. S. Bach

The question of temperament and the music of J. S. Bach (1685–1750) is complicated. Several writings on the subject will be reviewed.

No one in the eighteenth century attributed any temperament to Bach.[65]

Bach is said to have recommended tuning all major thirds "sharp"—that is, wider than pure. This means that a plan such as Kirnberger III with its pure major third C–E would be inconsistent with Bach's views.[66]

Bach's music does not seem to be "supported" by a single temperament. For example, both Ledbetter and Lindley believe that *The Well-Tempered Clavier* sounds better in an unequal temperament based on the fact that different key signatures are treated differently.[67] On the other hand, Lindley notes that the six-part Ricercar from *The Musical Offering* sounds better in equal temperament due to its use of D♭ in straightforward harmonies.[68]

The term "well-tempered" as used by Bach does not refer to a particular tuning[69] and may only mean "appropriately tuned" for the music at hand.[70]

Troeger asserts that Bach's use of enharmonic notes, "distant" key signatures such as F♯, and extensive modulations demonstrates that he expected a circulating temperament[71]—that is, one in which it is possible to modulate completely around the circle of fifths. Ledbetter believes that by the time of Book I of *The Well-Tempered Clavier* in 1722, Bach "seems to have moved towards something more evenly circulating" than Werckmeister III but in which "there is still a sensitivity to intervals and keys based on unequal tuning."[72] Lindley believes a subtle well-tempered system like Neidhardt's or Sorge's is probably most suitable;[73] these would be characterized by only a few pure fifths, tempered fifths of more than one size, and a narrow range of sizes for the major thirds. Temperaments with as many pure fifths as tempered fifths (Vallotti, Barnes, and Young no. 2) and those with more pure fifths than tempered fifths (Werckmeister III, Kirnberger III, and Kellner) may prove useful for the performance of Bach's music in a variety of circumstances but may be problematic in certain situations. The most important aspect of temperaments like Neidhardt's and Sorge's with respect to Bach's harmonic intricacies may be the absence of Pythagorean thirds.[74] In some cases, these intricacies make it difficult to completely dismiss equal temperament.

A recent area of interest is the hypothesis that the ornamental scroll at the top of the 1722 title page of *The Well-Tempered Clavier* is a diagrammatic representation of a well-tempered system. The idea was initially proposed by Andreas Sparschuh[75] with subsequent interpretations by Michael Zapf,[76] John Charles Francis,[77] Bradley Lehman,[78] and Daniel Jencka.[79] All these proposals tend toward a Neidhardt/Sorge type of subtlety.

An interesting perspective on the question of temperament and Bach is given by Peter Williams. In a discussion of *The Well-Tempered Clavier*, he mentions the unplayability of the ending of the A minor fugue from Book I, which leads him to the observations that "there are other things to do with music than play it or listen to it" and that in addition to playing and perceiving musical notes, J. S. Bach also thought and conceived musical ideas.[80] In other words, he believes that "J. S. Bach was not a composer to put player's convenience before the clear exposition of a musical concept"[81] and that the performer "should bear in mind the didactic or demonstrative nature of much of J. S. Bach's music."[82] By extension, he suggests this may be an approach to the temperament question: Bach may have been "concerned not with the empirical problem [of which temperament to use] but with the conceptual notion of using all the keys."[83] While this does not mean we should not play Bach's music when these practical problems are encountered, it does mean that our decision to play such music requires that we solve the problem ourselves, whether the notation is beyond the reach of the fingers, the music extends beyond the compass of our instrument, there is a scarcity of articulation marks, or organbuilders and harpsichordists must decide on a temperament for their respective instruments. Thus, the question "Which temperament is appropriate for the music of J. S. Bach?" may need to be approached as (a) improperly formulated, therefore (b) unanswerable, and so (c) a personal, interpretive (and, it is hoped, informed) choice.

Source of Confusion: Temperament Evolution

It is incorrect to establish a historical straight-line evolution of temperament from Pythagorean tuning or meantone temperament through the well-tempered systems to equal temperament.[84] The history of temperament involves several simultaneous lines of thought and practice, and at any particular time there would have been theorists and musicians with differing opinions. This is probably most true during the Baroque era. One should particularly avoid advancing the notion that equal temperament is the "ideal" toward which all historical discussions lead.

Summary

With its emphasis on pure major thirds, 1/4-comma meantone temperament began to be used during the second half of the fifteenth century—corresponding roughly to the start of the Renaissance—when the third became an important stable harmonic element. This is opposed to the use of Pythagorean tuning prior to the Renaissance, in which pure fifths were highly regarded and wide Pythagorean thirds were used as tension points that resolved to pure fifths. Extensive modulation to remote keys was being used well before the end of the Baroque era, which was about 1750; this caused problems with the use of meantone. However, publications advocating meantone temperament may be found later than 1800. Organs tended to remain in meantone-like temperaments, because it was a monumental task to re-tune an organ to a different temperament. The change away from meantone temperament in organs was after 1740 in north Germany and after 1850 in England.

Well-tempered systems began to appear by the late seventeenth century; Werckmeister's plan was first published in 1681 and may be regarded as the first documented temperament with no wolf interval. During the eighteenth century, the interval of a third was still considered an important harmonic element, but pure thirds were sacrificed for the ability to play in the more remote key signatures (keys with more than three sharps and two flats). As a result of different-size fifths and thirds, there was a distinct "character" to the different key signatures. The concept of key character persisted in some respects into the early nineteenth century.

The exact mathematics of equal-tempered semitones had been worked out by the sixteenth century, and approximations were used in the sixteenth century for the placement of frets on lutes and viols. There is no evidence Renaissance keyboard players used equal temperament. It was advocated by certain people in the seventeenth century, but the strongest arguments for its use began early in the eighteenth century. Near-equal temperaments were common in the nineteenth century.

While there are guidelines for the selection of a temperament, it may be impossible to correlate a particular piece of music with a particular temperament.

The question of which temperament to use for the music of J. S. Bach is complicated, but many of the characteristics of his music point to the necessity of at least a subtle, well-tempered system.

One should not assume a single evolutionary transition from Pythagorean tuning to meantone temperament to the well-tempered systems to equal temperament. One should also not assume that all paths lead to equal temperament.

Historical References

The references from the chronologies are included below for the sake of completeness, in chronological order. The information is derived from several sources.[85]

Ramos de Pareja, Bartolomeo. *Musica practica*. Bologna, 1482.

Schlick, Arnolt. *Spiegel der Orgelmacher und Organisten*. Speyer, 1511.

Aaron, Pietro. *Thoscanello de la musica*. Venice, 1523.

Zarlino, Gioseffo. *Le istitutioni harmoniche*. Venice, 1558.

————. *Dimostrationi harmoniche*. Venice, 1571.

Zhu Zaiyu. *Lü Li Jung-T'ung*. Completed 1581; published 1606.

Galilei, Vincenzo. *Dialogo della musica antica et della moderna*. Florence, 1581.

Stevin, Simon. *Vande Spiegheling der Singconst*. Unpublished, c1590s.

Praetorius, Michael. *Syntagma musicum. II: De organographia*. Wolfenbüttel, 1618.

Mersenne, Marin. *Harmonie universelle*. Paris, 1636–1637.

Rossi, Lemme. *Sistema musico, overo Musica speculativa*. Perugia, 1666.

Werckmeister, Andreas. *Orgel-Probe*. Frankfurt/Main, 1681.

————. *Musicalisches Temperatur*. Quedlinburg, 1691.

————. *Harmonologia musica*. Quedlinburg, 1702.

————. *Organum Gruningense redivivum*. Aschersleben, 1705.

Neidhardt, Johann Georg. *Beste und leichteste Temperatur des Monochordi*. Jena, 1706.

Sauveur, Joseph. "Méthode générale pour former les systèmes tempérés de musique, et du choix de celui qu'on doit suivre." *Histoire de l'Academie royale des sciences*, 1707. Paris, 1708.

————. "Table générale des systèmes tempérés." *Histoire de l'Academie royale des sciences*, 1711. Paris, 1714.

Neidhardt, Johann Georg. *Sectio canonis harmonici*. Königsberg, 1724.

Rameau, Jean-Philippe *Nouveau système de musique théorique*. Paris, 1726.

Neidhardt, Johann Georg *Gäntzlich erschöpfte mathematische Abtheilungen des diatonisch-chromatischen, temperirten Canonis Monochordi*. Leipzig/Königsberg, 1732.

Rameau, Jean Philippe. *Génération harmonique*. Paris, 1737.

Sorge, Georg Andreas. *Anweisung zur Stimmung und Temperatur in einem Gespräch*. Hamburg, 1744.

————. *Vorgemach der musicalishen Composition, II*. Lobenstein, 1746.

Tartini, Giuseppe. *Trattato di musica secondo la vera scienza dell' armonia*. Padua, 1754.

Marpurg, Friedrich Wilhelm. *Principes du clavecin*. Berlin, 1756.

Riccati, Giordano. *Saggio sopra le leggi del contrappunto*. Castelfranco, 1762.

Marpurg, Friedrich Wilhelm. *Versuch über die musikalische Temperatur*. Breslau, 1776.

Kirnberger, Johann Philipp. *Die Kunst des reinen Satzes in der Musik, II*. Berlin/Königsberg, 1776–1779.

Vallotti, Francesco Antonio. *Della scienza teorica e prattica della moderna musica*. Padua, 1779.

Cramer, C. F., ed., *Magazin de Musik ii.* Hamburg, 1784.

Encyclopedia Britannica, or a Dictionary of Arts, Sciences, and Miscellaneous Literature, 3rd ed. Edinburgh, 1797.

Young, Thomas. "Outlines of Experiments and Inquiries Respecting Sound and Light." *Philosophical Transactions of the Royal Society of London*, 90 (London, 1800): 106–50.

Hawkes, William. "On the Musical Temperament of Keyed Instruments." *The Philosophical Magazine* 28 (1807): 304–6.

Marsh, John. *A Short Introduction to the Theory of Harmonics, or the Philosophy of Musical Sounds.* London, 1809.

Notes

1. J. Murray Barbour, *Tuning and Temperament: A Historical Survey* (East Lansing: Michigan State College Press, 1951. Reprint, New York: DaCapo Press, 1972. Reprint, Mineola, N.Y.: Dover Publications, 2004); Mark Lindley, "Temperaments," in *The New Grove Dictionary of Musical Instruments*, 3 vols., ed. Stanley Sadie (London: Macmillan Press, 1984), 3:540–55; Mark Lindley, "Tuning and Intonation," in *Performance Practice: Music after 1600*. The Norton/Grove Handbooks in Music, ed. Howard Mayer Brown and Stanley Sadie (New York: W. W. Norton & Company, 1989), 169–85; and Rudolf Rasch, "Does 'Well-Tempered' Mean 'Equal-Tempered'?" in *Bach, Handel, Scarlatti: Tercentenary Essays*, ed. Peter Williams (Cambridge: Cambridge University Press, 1985), 293–310.

2. Lindley, "Temperaments," *New Grove*, 541.

3. Barbour, *Tuning and Temperament*, 10, 26; and Lindley, "Temperaments," *New Grove*, 541.

4. Lindley, "Temperaments," *New Grove*, 541; and Lindley, "Tuning and Intonation," 171.

5. Barbour, *Tuning and Temperament*, 27.

6. Lindley, "Temperaments," *New Grove*, 545.

7. Barbour, *Tuning and Temperament*, 28–29.

8. Lindley, "Temperaments," *New Grove*, 545.

9. Barbour, *Tuning and Temperament*, 35–36; and Lindley, "Temperaments," *New Grove*, 545.

10. Lindley, "Temperaments," *New Grove*, 545.

11. Lindley, "Temperaments," *New Grove*, 548; and Lindley, "Tuning and Intonation," 177–78.

12. Owen Jorgensen, *Tuning: Containing the Perfection of Eighteenth-Century Temperament, the Lost Art of Nineteenth-Century Temperament, and the Science of Equal Temperament, Complete with Instructions for Aural and*

Electronic Tuning (East Lansing: Michigan State University Press, 1991), 230–32, 298–300, 341–43.

13. Mark Lindley, "Some Thoughts Concerning the Effects of Tuning on Selected Musical Works (from Landini to Bach)," *Performance Practice Review* 9 (Spring 1996): 115.

14. Lindley, "Temperaments," *New Grove*, 541; and Lindley, "Tuning and Intonation," 170.

15. Lindley, "Temperaments," *New Grove*, 541.

16. Lindley, "Temperaments," *New Grove*, 542.

17. Lindley, "Temperaments," *New Grove*, 545.

18. Harald Vogel, "Tuning and Temperament in the North German School of the Seventeenth and Eighteenth Centuries," in *Charles Brenton Fisk, Organ Builder, Vol. I: Essays in His Honor*, ed. Fenner Douglass, Owen Jander, and Barbara Owen (Easthampton, Mass.: Westfield Center, 1986), 249.

19. Barbour, *Tuning and Temperament*, 10; and Lindley, "Temperaments," *New Grove*, 550.

20. Barbour, *Tuning and Temperament*, 137–38; Lindley, "Temperaments," *New Grove*, 543; and Lindley, "Tuning and Intonation," 178.

21. Lindley, "Temperaments," *New Grove*, 543; and Lindley, "Tuning and Intonation," 177, 179.

22. Rasch, "Does 'Well-Tempered' Mean 'Equal-Tempered'?" 294.

23. Rasch, "Does 'Well-Tempered' Mean 'Equal-Tempered'?" 298.

24. Lindley, "Tuning and Intonation," 180–81.

25. Lindley, "Temperaments," *New Grove*, 547.

26. Lindley, "Temperaments," *New Grove*, 548; and Lindley, "Tuning and Intonation," 184.

27. Lindley, "Some Thoughts," 115.

28. Lindley, "Temperaments," *New Grove*, 546.

29. Lindley, "Temperaments," *New Grove*, 547.

30. Lindley, "Temperaments," *New Grove*, 547; and Lindley, "Tuning and Intonation," 179.

31. Lindley, "Temperaments," *New Grove*, 549.

32. Lindley, "Temperaments," *New Grove*, 548.

33. Rita Steblin, *A History of Key Characteristics in the Eighteenth and Nineteenth Centuries*, 2nd ed. (Rochester, N.Y.: University of Rochester Press, 2002), 38, 90–92, 94–95, 188.

34. Gene Jinsiong Cho, *The Discovery of Musical Equal Temperament in China and Europe in the Sixteenth Century* (Lewiston, N.Y.: Edwin Mellen Press, 2003), 193–94.

35. Cho, *Discovery,* 195.

36. Barbour, *Tuning and Temperament*, 7–8, 57; Mark Lindley, *Lutes, Viols and Temperament* (Cambridge: Cambridge University Press, 1984), 20–21; Lindley, "Temperaments," *New Grove*, 544.

37. Barbour, *Tuning and Temperament*, 76; and Cho, *Discovery,* 218–26.

38. Cho, *Discovery,* 255–66.

39. Lindley, "Temperaments," *New Grove*, 544; and Lindley, "Tuning and Intonation," 175.

40. Lindley, "Temperaments," *New Grove*, 544; and Lindley, "Tuning and Intonation," 175–76.

41. Barbour, *Tuning and Temperament*, 79.

42. Rasch, "Does 'Well-Tempered' Mean 'Equal-Tempered'?" 298.

43. Rasch, "Does 'Well-Tempered' Mean 'Equal-Tempered'?" 300.

44. Lindley, "Tuning and Intonation," 181.

45. Lindley, "Temperaments," *New Grove*, 549.

46. Rasch, "Does 'Well-Tempered' Mean 'Equal-Tempered'?" 301.

47. Lindley, "Temperaments," *New Grove*, 550.

48. Lindley, "Some Thoughts," 115.

49. Lindley, *Lutes, Viols and Temperaments*, 19–21; and Lindley, "Temperaments," *New Grove*, 544.

50. Jorgensen, *Tuning*, 155–56; and Lindley, "Temperaments," *New Grove*, 544.

51. Lindley, "Tuning and Intonation," 180.

52. Lindley, "Temperaments," *New Grove*, 545.

53. Lindley, "Temperaments," *New Grove*, 549.

54. Lindley, "Temperaments," *New Grove*, 550.

55. Jorgensen, *Tuning*, 1–7.

56. Martin B. Tittle, *A Performer's Guide through Historical Keyboard Tunings*, rev. ed. (Ann Arbor, Mich.: Anderson Press, 1987), 39–57.

57. Claudio Di Veroli, *Unequal Temperaments and Their Role in the Performance of Early Music* (Buenos Aires: Artes Gráficas Farro, 1978), 136–37.

58. Di Veroli, *Unequal Temperaments*, 138.

59. Di Veroli, *Unequal Temperaments*, 136–56.

60. Richard Troeger, *Technique and Interpretation on the Harpsichord and Clavichord* (Bloomington: Indiana University Press, 1987), 207–17.

61. Troeger, *Technique and Interpretation*, 210.

62. Troeger, *Technique and Interpretation*, 209.

63. Troeger, *Technique and Interpretation*, 211.

64. Troeger, *Technique and Interpretation*, 209–10, 215.

65. Mark Lindley, "J. S. Bach's Tunings," *Musical Times* 126 (December 1986): 722.

66. Lindley, "J. S. Bach's Tunings," 721, 724; Lindley, "Tuning and Intonation," 183–84; and Rasch, "Does 'Well-Tempered' Mean 'Equal-Tempered'?" 302.

67. David Ledbetter, *Bach's* Well-Tempered Clavier*: The 48 Preludes and Fugues* (New Haven: Yale University Press, 2002), 156, 178, 192; and Lindley, "J. S. Bach's Tunings," 724.

68. Mark Lindley, "Temperaments," in *Oxford Composer Companions: J. S. Bach*, ed. Malcolm Boyd (Oxford: Oxford University Press, 1999), 476.

69. Mark Lindley, "Well-Tempered Clavier," in *The New Grove Dictionary of Musical Instruments*, ed. Stanley Sadie (London: Macmillan Press, 1984), 847.

70. Rasch, "Does 'Well-Tempered' Mean 'Equal-Tempered'?" 301.

71. Richard Troeger, *Playing Bach on the Keyboard: A Practical Guide* (Pompton Plains, N.J.: Amadeus Press, 2003), 255.

72. Ledbetter, *Bach's* Well-Tempered Clavier, 49–50.

73. Lindley, "J. S. Bach's Tunings," 722; and Lindley, "Well-Tempered Clavier," 848.

74. Ledbetter, *Bach's* Well-Tempered Clavier, 45, 207.

75. Andreas Sparschuh, "Stimm-Arithmetik des wohltemperierten Klaviers," *Deutsche Mathematiker Vereinigung Jahrestagung* (Mainz, 1999): 154–55.

76. Keith Briggs, "Letter to the Editor," *Early Music Review*, May 2003; and Clavichord Discussion Group, http://launch.groups.yahoo.com/group/clavichord/files (14 July 2005).

77. John Charles Francis, "Das Wohltemperirte Clavier: Pitch, Tuning, and Temperament Design," 2005, http://www.bach-cantatas.com/Articles/Das_Wohltemperirte_Clavier.htm (14 July 2005).

78. Bradley Lehman, "Bach's Extraordinary Temperament: Our Rosetta Stone–1." *Early Music* 33 (February 2005): 3–23; and Bradley Lehman, "Johann Sebastian Bach's Tuning," 2005, http://www.larips.com/ (11 February 2005).

79. Daniel Jencka, "J. S. Bach's Well-Tempered Clavier Tuning Script: A Proposed 1/18th PC Interpretation," 2005, http://bachtuning.jencka.com/essay.htm (14 July 2005).

80. Peter Williams, "J. S. Bach's Well-Tempered Clavier: A New Approach. 1," *Early Music* 11 (January 1983): 49.

81. Peter Williams, *The Organ Music of J. S. Bach, Vol. III: A Background* (Cambridge: Cambridge University Press, 1984), 195.

82. Williams, *The Organ Music of J. S. Bach, Vol. III*, 191.

83. Williams, "J. S. Bach's Well-Tempered Clavier, 1", 49.

84. Di Veroli, *Unequal Temperaments*, 135.

85. Lindley, "Temperaments," *New Grove*, 552–55; Manuel Op de Coul et al., "Tuning and Temperament Bibliography," 2003, http://www.xs4all.nl/~huygensf/doc/bib.html (7 September 2003); Don Michael Randel, ed., *The Harvard Biographical Dictionary of Music* (Cambridge, Mass.: The Belknap Press of Harvard University Press, 1996); Rasch, "Does 'Well-Tempered' Mean 'Equal-Tempered'?" 309–10; and Steblin, *A History of Key Characteristics*, 373–93.

Part 2
Supplementary Material

8

Starting Notes, Pitch References, and Transposition

One way to set a tempered interval is according to the number of beats per second. Recall that beats are dependent on frequency; so, for any given tempered interval with a specific beat rate, the same interval an octave higher beats twice as fast. This prompts two questions. What is the effect of different starting notes on beat rates? What is the effect of the same beat rate used at different pitch references (A440 vs. A415 vs. A392)?

Starting Notes

The starting note—the pitch from which one lays the bearings—may be any note, but is typically A or C. The problem is that tuning forks are based on equal-tempered semitones, which could be incompatible with the unequal temperament at hand. That is, an unequal temperament set from an A440 tuning fork would have a C frequency different from a C523.3 tuning fork. Likewise, the same temperament set from a C523.3 tuning fork would have an A frequency different from an A440 tuning fork. So for any given temperament—other than equal temperament—the series of frequencies calculated from A would not match the series of frequencies calculated from C. If the frequencies are different, then the beat rates will also be different. Therefore, we need to examine the difference between A-based and C-based beat rates and the significance of that difference. Based on the method in chapter 4, the tenor frequencies and the beat rates of the fifths are calculated for 1/4-comma meantone temperament and Vallotti from two different starting notes, based on A440 and C523.3 tuning forks (tables 8.1 and 8.2).

Table 8.1. Frequencies and Beat Rates of Fifths for 1/4-Comma Meantone Temperament at Two Different Starting Notes

Note	A440 Frequencies	Beat Rates of Fifths	C523.3 Frequencies	Beat Rates of Fifths
c	131.5907	−1.2241	**130.8250**	−1.2170
c♯	137.5000	−1.2791	136.6999	−1.2716
d	147.1229	−1.3686	146.2668	−1.3606
e♭	157.4192	−1.4644	156.5032	−1.4559
e	164.4884	−1.5301	163.5312	−1.5212
f	176.0000	−1.6372	174.9759	−1.6277
f♯	183.9036	−1.7108	182.8335	−1.7008
g	196.7740	−1.8305	195.6290	−1.8198
g♯	205.6105	12.8454	204.4141	12.7706
a	**220.0000**	−2.0465	218.7199	−2.0346
b♭	235.3966	−2.1898	234.0269	−2.1770
b	245.9675	−2.2881	244.5363	−2.2748
c^l	263.1814	−2.4482	**261.6500**	−2.4340

Table 8.2. Frequencies and Beat Rates of Fifths for Vallotti Temperament at Two Different Starting Notes

Note	A440 Frequencies	Beat Rates of Fifths	C523.3 Frequencies	Beat Rates of Fifths
c	131.2567	−0.8883	**130.8250**	−0.8854
c♯	138.5913	0.0000	138.1355	0.0000
d	146.9983	−0.9949	146.5148	−0.9916
e♭	155.9152	0.0000	155.4024	0.0000
e	164.6278	−1.1142	164.0863	−1.1105
f	175.4046	−1.1871	174.8277	−1.1832
f♯	184.7884	0.0000	184.1807	0.0000
g	196.4409	−1.3295	195.7948	−1.3251
g♯	207.8870	0.0000	207.2032	0.0000
a	**220.0000**	−1.4889	219.2764	−1.4840
b	233.8728	0.0000	233.1037	0.0000
b♭	246.3846	0.0000	245.5742	0.0000
c^l	262.5134	−1.7767	**261.6500**	−1.7708

A mention should be made of the pitch-reference frequencies. The designations "A440," "A415," and "A392" are commonly used approximations based on the frequencies of equal-tempered tuning forks. The precise equal-tempered frequencies based on 440.0000 Hz would actually be 415.3047 Hz and 391.9954 Hz. Here, we will use the rounded values of 415.3 Hz and 392.0 Hz. For a "C523" pitch reference, the rounded value used is 523.3 Hz.

Notice that the beat rates are slightly different for each temperament between the two different starting pitches. For 1/4-comma meantone temperament, the difference is 0.58 percent; for example, for c–g: –1.2241 vs. –1.2170. For Vallotti, the difference is 0.33 percent; for example, for c–g: –0.8883 vs. –0.8854. These differences are negligible. Whether one uses either A or C for a starting note at the A440 pitch level—even with the use of equal tempered tuning forks—there is no practical difference in the beat rates. The same holds true for A and C starting notes at the A415 pitch level, which would be calculated based on a G♯415.3 tuning fork and a B493.9 tuning fork respectively.

Pitch References

The next question is whether we can use A440 beat rates at an A415 or A392 pitch reference or whether we need separate sets of beat rates. To examine this, we will use the Vallotti tuning instructions from chapter 6 and a pitch reference of A415. Two sets of frequencies are calculated: one using A440 beat rates and the other using A415 beat rates. A415 beat rates are generated from A440 beat rates by multiplying the latter by 0.9438743 as described in chapter 4. Since it was noted above that differences between A- and C-based frequency sets are negligible, we will use just the A-based frequencies. (The value used for the A415 pitch reference is 207.6500 Hz, which is based on a rounded a^1 equal-tempered frequency of 415.3 Hz.) In table 8.3, the first column corresponds to the sequence of steps in the tuning instructions, with the note in bold type indicating the frequency being calculated. The method of calculating frequencies from beat rates is described in chapter 4. The differences in the A415 beat-rate frequencies in relation to the A440 beat-rate frequencies—column 5 relative to column 3 in table 8.3—are shown in table 8.4. The differences are negligible. Tables 8.5 and 8.6 give data for Vallotti using A440 and A392 beat rates at an A392 pitch

Table 8.3. Vallotti Tenor Frequencies: A415 Pitch Reference, A440 vs. A415 Beat Rates

Interval or Note	A440 Beat Rate	Frequency	A415 Beat Rate	Frequency
a	——	**207.6500**	——	**207.6500**
f–a	+2.9768	165.5246	+2.8097	165.5581
f–c¹	−1.1871	247.6934	−1.1205	247.7768
f–b♭	0	220.6995	0	220.7441
e♭–b♭	0	147.1330	0	147.1627
e♭–g♯	0	196.1774	0	196.2170
c♯–g♯	0	130.7849	0	130.8113
c♯–f♯	0	174.3799	0	174.4151
f♯–b	0	232.5065	0	232.5534
e–b	−1.1142	155.3757	−1.0516	155.3862
d–b	+4.1622	138.6715	+3.9286	138.7463
c–g	−0.8883	185.3259	−0.8385	185.4134

Table 8.4. Frequency Differences from Table 8.3

Note	Hz Diff.	Cent Diff.	% Diff.
a	0	0	0
f	+0.033 Hz	+0.350 ¢	+0.020 %
c¹	+0.083	+0.583	+0.034
b♭	+0.045	+0.350	+0.020
e♭	+0.030	+0.350	+0.020
g♯	+0.040	+0.350	+0.020
c♯	+0.026	+0.350	+0.020
f♯	+0.035	+0.350	+0.020
b	+0.047	+0.350	+0.020
e	+0.010	+0.116	+0.007
d	+0.075	+0.935	+0.054
g	+0.087	+0.817	+0.047

Table 8.5. Vallotti Tenor Frequencies: A392 Pitch Reference, A440 vs. A392
Beat Rates

Interval or Note	A440 Beat Rate	Frequency	A392 Beat Rate	Frequency
a	——	**196.0000**	——	**196.0000**
f–a	+2.9768	156.2046	+2.6520	156.2696
f–c¹	−1.1871	233.7134	−1.0576	233.8756
f–b♭	0	208.2729	0	208.3595
e♭–b♭	0	138.8486	0	138.9063
e♭–g#	0	185.1314	0	185.2084
c#–g#	0	123.4210	0	123.4723
c#–f#	0	164.5613	0	164.6297
f#–b	0	219.4150	0	219.5063
e–b	−1.1142	146.6481	−0.9926	146.6684
d–b	+4.1622	130.8166	+3.7081	130.9621
c–g	0.8883	174.8409	−0.7914	175.0110

Table 8.6. Frequency Differences from Table 8.5

Note	Hz Diff.	Cent Diff.	% Diff.
a	0	0	0
f	+0.065 Hz	+0.720 ¢	+0.042 %
c¹	+0.162	+1.201	+0.069
b♭	+0.087	+0.720	+0.042
e♭	+0.058	+0.720	+0.042
g#	+0.077	+0.720	+0.042
c#	+0.051	+0.720	+0.042
f#	+0.068	+0.720	+0.042
b	+0.091	+0.720	+0.042
e	+0.020	+0.240	+0.014
d	+0.146	+1.925	+0.111
g	+0.170	+1.683	+0.097

reference. (A440 beat rates multiplied by 0.8908987 yield A392 beat rates.) Again, the differences are slight. So, the use of a single set of beat rates is acceptable for different pitch references. The differences are least for a one-semitone change, such as A440 beat rates at A415. The differences are slightly greater for a two-semitone change, such as A440 beat rates at A392. If A392 is the pitch reference of choice, one may want to consider doing all calculations based on that pitch reference.

Transposition

The topic of transposition in relation to temperament will be briefly addressed with regard to two subjects: transposing keyboards and transposed fifth patterns.

A transposing keyboard is found on many harpsichords and continuo organs. This is a design feature that allows the keyboard to be shifted to the left or right one or two semitones (more specifically, one or two key-end widths). Its purpose is to allow the instrument to be used at different pitch levels without re-tuning the strings or the pipes the distance of a semitone or a whole tone. The three most common pitch levels used are A392, A415, and A440.

Unfortunately, most temperaments do not transpose well, especially one semitone up or down. Since many temperaments have a certain fifth pattern that results in a particular character to the major thirds, semitones, and key signatures, transposing this pattern alters its character. With a temperament set, shifting the keyboard down one semitone means that the C string is now activated by the C♯ key; the fifth pattern has been shifted almost halfway around the circle of fifths. For example, the fifth pattern of Werckmeister III according to the circle of fifths is

6 6 6 0   0 **6** 0 0   0 0 0 0

with the bold type indicating the fifth on C tempered 6 cents narrower than pure. Shifting the keyboard down one semitone is the same as if one set the temperament from the note C♯:

6 0 0 0   0 0 0 **6**   **6** 6 0 0.

With non-transposed Werckmeister III, the purer major thirds are on F and C and the wider Pythagorean thirds are on F♯, C♯, and G♯. With the transposed version, the purer major thirds are on F♯ and C♯, and the Pythagorean thirds are on G, D, and A. This is a major alteration of the temperament's character. A less dramatic change would be to shift the keyboard *two* semitones or a major second, which changes it from C-based to either B♭-based or D-based. Transpositions of two semitones or a major second were historically more common because they accommodated the relationship of keyboard temperaments with other instruments better than semitone transpositions.[1]

The only temperament that is perfectly transposable is equal temperament, because every fifth is the same size, and every major third is the same size. Transposable unequal temperaments are possible;[2] they need to have symmetrical fifth patterns that cut the circle of fifths in half, such as

6 6 0 0   0 0 6 6   0 0 0 0   or   4 4 4 0   0 0 4 4   4 0 0 0.

With such plans, a transposition of one semitone would not affect the major thirds too much. However, these symmetrical patterns are quite different from the classic temperament plans. In some ways, a transposable temperament is only of consequence for continuo organs, which generally do not need to be constantly tuned by the performer. For harpsichords, one would shift the transposing keyboard, use the proper tuning fork for the new pitch level, and simply adjust the pitches to the desired temperament, since the instrument would need tuning anyway.

Source of Confusion:
Starting Notes vs. Transposition

The starting note is the pitch from which one lays the bearings. Many tuning instructions traditionally used C as a starting note (for whatever reasons). On the other hand, once the pitch reference of a^l = 440 Hz was established, there was a strong impetus to use A as a starting note. The important point is that the pattern of fifths—that is, which fifths are pure and which fifths are tempered—is the same for any given temperament, whether one uses C or A for the starting note. One may set a temperament by starting on either a C or an A, but the different starting note does not change the pattern of tempered fifths.

The transposition of a temperament refers to the fact that the pure and tempered fifths are in the same pattern, but that pattern is shifted. This is analogous to taking a piece of music written in the key of C and transposing it into the key of D. Once a temperament is transposed, the transposed version may be set from either A or C, just as the non-transposed version may be set from either A or C.

Notes

1. Bruce Haynes, *A History of Performing Pitch: The Story of "A"* (Lanham, Md.: Scarecrow Press, 2002), xxxv, liv, 191.

2. Thomas Donahue, "A Transposable Temperament," *Diapason* 89 (March 1998): 12.

9

Theoretical and
Equal-Beating Versions

This chapter examines the distinctions between the theoretical and the equal-beating versions of a temperament.

Table 9.1 presents the theoretical version of Vallotti in a specific way: the frequencies of the tenor octave (*c* to *b*) are given with theoretical beat rates, calculated according to the instructions for laying the bearings from chapter 6. The values were calculated using the methods and equations given in chapter 4.

Table 9.2 presents the temperings of the theoretical version of Vallotti. The cent values in this table were calculated from the frequencies in table 9.1: the frequencies were compiled as frequency ratios of the fifths in the circle of fifths and converted to cent values using the cent equation given in chapter 1. For completeness, the temperings are given in three different ways, as in chapter 2.

Table 9.3 presents an equal-beating version of Vallotti according to the tuning instructions given by Jorgensen.[1] Table 9.4 presents the temperings of this equal-beating version derived from those frequencies.

Compared to the theoretical tempering of −4 cents or −1/6 PC, the tempering of the fifths in the equal-beating version varies from −2.9 to −4.9 cents, or approximately −1/8 PC to −1/5 PC. Thus, the intervals that are tempered in the equal-beating manner vary considerably from the theoretical; in the case of Vallotti, this involves four of the six fifth intervals. However, the sizes of the major thirds are essentially the same between the two versions, as shown in table 9.5. The reason for the similarity of the major thirds even though the equal-beating fifths deviate quite a bit from the theoretical is because a major third is derived from four fifths, and this allows the deviations of the fifths to be averaged out.

Table 9.1. Theoretical Version of Vallotti, Precise Beat Rates

Interval	Note Tuned	Beat Rate	Frequency
——	*a*	——	220.0000
f–a	*f*	+2.9768	175.4046
f–c¹	*c¹*	−1.1871	262.5134
f–b♭	*b♭*	0	233.8729
e♭–b♭	*e♭*	0	155.9152
e♭–g♯	*g♯*	0	207.8870
c♯–g♯	*c♯*	0	138.5913
c♯–f♯	*f♯*	0	184.7884
f♯–b	*b*	0	246.3846
e–b	*e*	−1.1142	164.6278
d–b	*d*	+4.1622	146.9983
c–g	*g*	−0.8883	196.4409

Table 9.2. Fifth Tempering in Theoretical Version of Vallotti

Interval	Cents	Comma	Tempering
C–G	698	−4	−1/6 PC
G–D	698	−4	−1/6 PC
D–A	698	−4	−1/6 PC
A–E	698	−4	−1/6 PC
E–B	698	−4	−1/6 PC
B–F♯	702	0	pure
F♯–C♯	702	0	pure
C♯–G♯	702	0	pure
G♯–E♭	702	0	pure
E♭–B♭	702	0	pure
B♭–F	702	0	pure
F–C	698	−4	−1/6 PC

Table 9.3. Equal-Beating Version of Vallotti

Interval	Note Tuned	Beat Rate	Frequency
——	*a*	——	220.0000
d–a	*d*	−1.1	147.0333
d–g	*g*	+1.1	196.4111
c–g	*c*	−1.1	131.3074
e–a	*e*	+1.1	164.7250
e–b	*b*	−1.1	246.5375
f♯–b	*f♯*	0	184.9031
c♯–f♯	*c♯*	0	138.6773
c♯–g♯	*g♯*	0	208.0160
e♭–g♯	*e♭*	0	156.0120
e♭–b♭	*b♭*	0	234.0180
f–b♭	*f*	0	175.5135

Table 9.4. Fifth Tempering in Equal-Beating Version of Vallotti

Interval	Cents	Comma	Tempering
C–G	697.1	−4.9	−1/5 PC
G–D	698.7	−3.3	−1/7 PC
D–A	697.6	−4.4	−1/5 PC
A–E	699.1	−2.9	−1/8 PC
E–B	698.1	−3.9	−1/6 PC
B–F♯	702	0	pure
F♯–C♯	702	0	pure
C♯–G♯	702	0	pure
G♯–E♭	702	0	pure
E♭–B♭	702	0	pure
B♭–F	702	0	pure
F–C	697.6	−4.4	−1/6 PC

Chapter 9

Table 9.5. Vallotti Major Thirds, Theoretical vs. Equal-Beating, in Cents

	Theoretical		Equal-Beating	
Interval	Size	Dev.[a]	Size	Dev.[a]
C–E	392.2	6.2	392.5	6.5
G–B	392.2	6.2	393.5	7.5
D–F♯	396.1	10.1	396.8	10.8
A–C♯	400.0	14.0	401.1	15.1
E–G♯	403.9	17.9	404.0	18.0
B–E♭	407.8	21.8	407.8	21.8
F♯–B♭	407.8	21.8	407.8	21.8
C♯–F	407.8	21.8	407.8	21.8
G♯–C	403.9	17.9	403.5	17.5
E♭–G	400.0	14.0	398.7	12.7
B♭–D	396.1	10.1	395.4	9.4
F–A	392.2	6.2	391.1	5.1

a. Deviation in cents from a pure major third of 386 cents

Note

1. Owen Jorgensen, *Tuning: Containing the Perfection of Eighteenth-Century Temperament, the Lost Art of Nineteenth-Century Temperament, and the Science of Equal Temperament, Complete with Instructions for Aural and Electronic Tuning* (East Lansing: Michigan State University Press, 1991), 68–72.

10

Near-Equal Temperament

Equal temperament is a difficult temperament to set. This is evident when one looks at the beat rates for the fifths, fourths, and major thirds (table 10.1). There are no pure intervals, and there is only one interval in the tenor octave with a whole-number beat rate. The typical way to set equal temperament is to temper all the fifths very slightly in such a way that any given third beats faster that the one below it and slower than the one above it (as illustrated in column four). This takes considerable experience to master.

Table 10.1. Beat Rates for Equal Temperament, Tenor Octave

Root Note	Fifths	Fourths	Major Thirds
c	−0.4	0.6	5.2
c♯	−0.5	0.6	5.5
d	−0.5	0.7	5.8
e♭	−0.5	0.7	6.2
e	−0.6	0.7	6.5
f	−0.6	0.8	6.9
f♯	−0.6	0.8	7.3
g	−0.7	0.9	7.8
g♯	−0.7	0.9	8.2
a	−0.7	1.0	8.7
b♭	−0.8	1.1	9.2
b	−0.8	1.1	9.8
c¹	−0.9	1.2	10.4

This chapter presents an alternate temperament that is close to equal temperament but easier to set by ear. This is only one of many; the subject of equal and near-equal temperaments has been discussed extensively by Jorgensen.[1]

The temperament, called "Neidhardt Quasi-Equal Temperament" by Jorgensen, was published by Johann Georg Neidhardt in 1732 and was referred to as Fifth temperament no. 3.[2] The layout of the fifths is shown in table 10.2.

Table 10.2. Fifths in Neidhardt's Fifth Temperament No. 3

Interval	Tempering	Cents	Comma
C–G	pure	702	0
G–D	–1/6 PC	698	–4
D–A	pure	702	0
A–E	–1/6 PC	698	–4
E–B	pure	702	0
B–F♯	–1/6 PC	698	–4
F♯–C♯	pure	702	0
C♯–G♯	–1/6 PC	698	–4
G♯–E♭	pure	702	0
E♭–B♭	–1/6 PC	698	–4
B♭–F	pure	702	0
F–C	–1/6 PC	698	–4

The concept of this temperament is to temper six fifths by one-sixth of the Pythagorean comma, keep the other six fifths pure, and alternate the two types of fifths. The result is only one size major third—400 cents—the same size as in equal temperament. Consequently, the classic progression of beat rates of the major thirds in equal temperament is maintained in this near-equal temperament. The semitones are two sizes, either 98 or 102 cents.

Here is a method to set this temperament.

Neidhardt's Fifth Temperament No. 3

from a
tune **a** to pitch
tune pure: **d**–a, d–**d**^{1}
temper d–**g** wider than pure, 1 beat per second (+1.3)
tune pure: **c**–g, c–**c**^{1}
temper c–**e** wider than pure, 5 beats per second (+5.2)
tune pure: e–**b**
temper c–**f** wider than pure, to beat as d–g (+1.2 vs. +1.3)
check: f–a (+6.9) beats as f–d^1 (+6.9) and c–a (+6.7)
tune pure: f–**b**♭
temper **c**♯–f wider than pure to beat as c–e (+5.5 vs. +5.2)
tune pure: c♯–**f**♯
temper **e**♭–b♭ to beat as f–c^1 (–1.1 vs. –1.2)
tune pure: e♭–**g**♯
range: c–c^1, plus d^1
from c
tune **c** to pitch
tune pure: c–**g**, c–**c**^{1}
temper c–**e** wider than pure, 5 beats per second (+5.2)
tune pure: e–**b**
temper c–**f** wider than pure, 1 beat per second (+1.2)
tune pure: f–**b**♭
temper **c**♯–f wider than pure to beat as c–e (+5.5 vs. +5.2)
tune pure: c♯–**f**♯
temper **e**♭–b♭ to beat as f–c^1 (–1.1 vs. –1.2)
tune pure: e♭–**g**♯
temper **d**–g wider than pure to beat as c–f (+1.3 vs. +1.2)
tune pure: d–**a**
range: c–c^1

This temperament has five tempering steps, placing its degree of difficulty on par with Vallotti, Young no. 2, and Barnes (see table 6.1).

Notes

1. Owen Jorgensen, *Tuning: Containing the Perfection of Eighteenth-Century Temperament, the Lost Art of Nineteenth-Century Temperament, and the Science of Equal Temperament, Complete with Instructions for Aural and Electronic Tuning* (East Lansing: Michigan State University Press, 1991), 352–711.

2. J. Murray Barbour, *Tuning and Temperament: A Historical Survey* (East Lansing: Michigan State College Press, 1951. Reprint, New York: DaCapo Press, 1972. Reprint, Mineola, N.Y.: Dover Publications, 2004), 164; and Jorgensen, *Tuning,* 473–78.

11

Derivation of the Cent Equation

The following explanation of the cent equation is based on the material presented by Backus.[1]

The frequency ratio for the octave is 2:1, meaning the frequency of the higher note is twice the frequency of the lower note in the interval. For simplicity, we will use the numbers 1 and 2 as the frequencies for a low C and a high C respectively. Assuming equal temperament—in which all semitones are the same size—we will use the letter x to represent the decimal value of the equal-tempered semitone.

With the frequency of low C as 1, we find the frequency of C♯ by multiplying 1 by the decimal value of the semitone, that is, $1 \times x$, which is simply x. To find the frequency of D, we multiply the frequency of C♯ by x, which is $x \times x$, or x^2. To find the frequency of E♭, we multiply the frequency of D by x, which is $x^2 \times x$, or x^3. The frequencies of all the notes in the octave calculated by this method are

C: 1	E: x^4	G♯: x^8	C: x^{12}
C♯: x	F: x^5	A: x^9	
D: x^2	F♯: x^6	B♭: x^{10}	
E♭: x^3	G: x^7	B: x^{11}	

Since the frequency of the high C note is twice the frequency of the low C, the frequency of the high C may be written as either x^{12} or 2. Since these two values are equivalent, we can write

$$x^{12} = 2.$$

Now we can solve for x by taking the twelfth root of both sides:

$$\sqrt[12]{x^{12}} = \sqrt[12]{2} \;, \qquad x = \sqrt[12]{2} \;,$$

which is equivalent to

$$x = 2^{1/12}.$$

The value of x is 1.059463094. This number—the twelfth root of 2—is the multiplier one uses to calculate equal-tempered semitones. If the actual frequency of C is 261.63 Hz, then the frequency of C♯ is

$$261.63 \times 1.059463094 = 277.19 \text{ Hz}.$$

To find the frequency of G—which is x^7—the calculation is

$$261.63 \times (1.059463094)^7 = 392.00 \text{ Hz}.$$

We now use the concept of cents. It has already been (arbitrarily) decided that each equal-tempered semitone is 100 cents. This means that one cent is 1/100 of a semitone. Since the semitone multiplier x can be multiplied by itself twelve times to find out the value of the octave (x^{12}), the cent value can be multiplied by itself one hundred times to find out the value of the semitone multiplier x. If c is the cent multiplier, c^{100} is the value of a semitone and this is equivalent to x. So,

$$c^{100} = x.$$

Since $x = 2^{1/12}$,

$$c^{100} = 2^{1/12}.$$

Taking the one-hundreth root of each side allows us to solve for c:

$$\sqrt[100]{c^{100}} = \sqrt[100]{2^{1/12}} \;, \qquad c = 2^{1/1200}.$$

The cent multiplier c is analogous to the semitone multiplier x calculated above. We actually have very little use for a cent multiplier, so the actual value of c is unimportant. But the above equation is useful because with it we can derive the equation for the relationship between frequency ratios and cents. We can make the equation for the cent multiplier more general. For any interval that is N cents, the equation becomes

$$c^N = 2^{N/1200}.$$

To find out what c^N represents, take the following example. We calculated above that the semitone multiplier for G above C was x^7, with x = 1.059463094. If the frequency of C is 261.63 Hz, then the frequency of G is

$$261.63 \times (1.059463094)^7 = 392.00 \text{ Hz}.$$

Since we defined that a semitone is 100 cents, the interval C–G—which is seven semitones—is 700 cents. Using this for the value of N, we find

$$c^{700} = 2^{700/1200} = 1.4983.$$

This number represents the frequency ratio of the interval C–G, or the frequency of G divided by the frequency of C; that is,

$$392.00 \div 261.63 = 1.4983.$$

So in general terms, the quantity c^N is the frequency ratio (in decimal form) of the interval of N cents. Therefore we can write

$$\text{frequency ratio} = 2^{N/1200}.$$

Letting R stand for the frequency ratio and taking the logarithm of each side gives

$$\log R = \log\left(2^{N/1200}\right).$$

Since $\log a^b = b \log a$ (with "a" being 2 and "b" being N/1200), we can write

$$\log R = \frac{N}{1200} \log 2 \,.$$

Solving for N yields

$$N = 1200 \frac{\log R}{\log 2} \,.$$

Dividing 1200 by log 2 simplifies the equation to

$$N = 3986 \log R.$$

Since N represents cents and R represents the frequency ratio, the equation may be written

cents = 3986 log (frequency ratio).

It should be mentioned for the sake of completeness that the actual value of 1200 divided by log 2 is 3986.31371386483.

To find the cent value of any interval when the frequencies of the two notes are known, divide the higher frequency by the lower frequency, take the logarithm, and multiply by 3986. For example:

Frequency no. 1 = 327.88 Hertz
Frequency no. 2 = 261.63 Hertz
Frequency ratio = 327.88 ÷ 261.63 = 1.25322
3986 log (1.25322) = 391 cents.

An alternate form of the equation is

$$\text{frequency ratio} = 10^{(\text{cent value} \div 3986)}$$

which may be used to find the frequency ratio of an interval whose cent value is known. If a fifth is tempered by one-quarter of the syntonic comma (or 5.5 cents), the size of such a fifth is calculated by subtracting the tempering from the cent value of a pure fifth, 702 cents. That is,

702 − 5.5 = 696.5 cents.

The frequency ratio is calculated from this value in the following way:

$$\text{frequency ratio} = 10^{(696.5 \div 3986)} = 1.495328387.$$

While such a calculation looks intimidating, it is easily done on a scientific calculator with a 10^X key. The key sequence is: 696.5, $\div$, 3986, =, 10^X. This value for the frequency ratio may now be used to calculate actual frequencies for a temperament (see chapter 4).

Note

1. John Backus, *The Acoustical Foundations of Music*, 2nd ed. (New York, W. W. Norton & Company, 1977), 146–47, 349–50.

12

Temperament Data

The description of the temperaments in chapter 2 presented three ways of characterizing the sizes of the fifths. It is also possible to characterize each temperament in other ways, in terms of the chromatic scale from C to C. Each of the tables 12.1 through 12.17 includes the following additional numerical information about the temperaments discussed in this book, for the notes in the tenor octave from c to c^{l}:

1. Frequencies, in Hz. Both A-based and C-based frequencies are given, calculated with precise values for frequency ratios as given in chapter 4. For the C-based frequencies, the reference pitch is not taken from a rounded value from a tuning fork—that is, not

$$523.3 \div 2 = 261.65 \text{ Hz}$$

but rather it is calculated with the equal-tempered semitone multiplier 1.059463094 from $a = 220$ Hz; that is,

$$220 \times (1.059463094)^3 = 261.6256 \text{ Hz}.$$

2. Deviation from equal-tempered frequencies, in cents. Both A-based and C-based values are given. A negative sign indicates a frequency that is lower than its equal-tempered counterpart.
3. Cumulative cent values. With these values, c is always 0 and c^{l} is always 1200.
4. Size of the semitones, in cents. Each value is measured between the given note and the adjacent lower note.
5. Beat rates for fifths, fourths, major thirds, minor thirds, and major sixths, in beats per second. A negative sign indicates the interval is narrower than pure.

The frequencies and the beat rates would be twice as much for the octave above (c^1 to c^2) and half as much for the octave below (C to c). The cent values are the same regardless of the octave.

At the end of the chapter, there is a discussion of the question of the compatibility of temperaments with bowed string instruments.

Table 12.1. Pythagorean Tuning

Note	A440 Frequency	A440 ET Dev.	A523.3 Frequency	A523.3 ET Dev.	Cumu- lative	Semi- tones
c	130.3704	−5.9	**130.8128**	0.0	0	0
c#	139.2188	7.8	139.6912	13.7	114	114
d	146.6667	−2.0	147.1644	3.9	204	90
e♭	154.5130	−11.7	155.0374	−5.9	294	90
e	165.0000	2.0	165.5599	7.8	408	114
f	173.8272	−7.8	174.4170	−2.0	498	90
f#	185.6250	5.9	186.2549	11.7	612	114
g	195.5556	−3.9	196.2192	2.0	702	90
g#	208.8281	9.8	209.5368	15.6	816	114
a	**220.0000**	0.0	220.7466	5.9	906	90
b♭	231.7695	−9.8	232.5561	−3.9	996	90
b	247.5000	3.9	248.3399	9.8	1110	114
c¹	260.7407	−5.9	**261.6256**	0.0	1200	90

BEAT RATES

Note	5ths	4ths	M3rds	m3rds	M6ths
c	0.0	0.0	8.1	−9.7	8.1
c#	0.0	0.0	−0.8	−10.3	−0.8
d	0.0	0.0	9.2	−10.9	9.2
e♭	0.0	8.4	9.7	1.0	9.7
e	0.0	0.0	10.3	−12.2	10.3
f	0.0	0.0	10.9	1.2	10.9
f#	0.0	0.0	−1.0	−13.8	−1.0
g	0.0	0.0	12.2	−14.5	12.2
g#	-8.4	0.0	−1.2	−15.5	−1.2
a	0.0	0.0	13.8	−16.3	13.8
b♭	0.0	0.0	14.5	1.6	14.5
b	0.0	0.0	−1.4	−18.3	15.5
c¹	0.0	0.0	16.3	−19.3	16.3

Table 12.2. 1/4-Comma Meantone Temperament

Note	A440 Frequency	A440 ET Dev.	A523.3 Frequency	A523.3 ET Dev.	Cumu-lative	Semi-tones
c	131.5907	10.3	**130.8128**	**0.0**	0	0
c♯	137.5000	-13.7	136.6872	-23.9	76	76
d	147.1229	3.4	146.2531	-6.8	193	117
e♭	157.4192	20.5	156.4886	10.3	310	117
e	164.4884	-3.4	163.5160	-13.7	386	76
f	176.0000	13.7	174.9596	3.4	503	117
f♯	183.9036	-10.3	182.8164	-20.5	579	76
g	196.7740	6.8	195.6107	-3.4	697	117
g♯	205.6105	-17.1	204.3950	-27.4	773	76
a	**220.0000**	**0.0**	218.6995	-10.3	890	117
b♭	235.3966	17.1	234.0050	6.8	1007	117
b	245.9675	-6.8	244.5134	-17.1	1083	76
c¹	263.1814	10.3	**261.6256**	**0.0**	1200	117

BEAT RATES

Note	5ths	4ths	M3rds	m3rds	M6ths
c	-1.2	1.6	0.0	-2.4	2.0
c♯	-1.3	1.7	16.5	-2.6	18.7
d	-1.4	1.8	0.0	-2.7	2.3
e♭	-1.5	-12.8	0.0	-25.0	2.4
e	-1.5	2.0	0.0	-3.1	2.6
f	-1.6	2.2	0.0	-27.9	2.7
f♯	-1.7	2.3	22.1	-3.4	25.0
g	-1.8	2.4	0.0	-3.7	3.1
g♯	12.8	·2.6	24.7	-3.8	27.9
a	-2.0	2.7	0.0	-4.1	3.4
b♭	-2.2	2.9	0.0	-37.4	3.7
b	-2.3	3.1	29.5	-4.6	3.8
c¹	-2.4	3.3	0.0	-4.9	4.1

Table 12.3. Werckmeister III

Note	A440 Frequency	A440 ET Dev.	A523.3 Frequency	A523.3 ET Dev.	Cumu- lative	Semi- tones
c	131.7021	11.7	**130.8128**	**0.0**	0	0
c#	138.7479	2.0	137.8110	−9.8	90	90
d	147.1644	3.9	146.1706	−7.8	192	102
e♭	156.0914	5.9	155.0374	−5.9	294	102
e	165.0000	2.0	163.8858	−9.8	390	96
f	175.6028	9.8	174.4170	−2.0	498	108
f#	184.9972	0.0	183.7480	−11.7	588	90
g	196.8850	7.8	195.5556	−3.9	696	108
g#	208.1219	3.9	206.7165	−7.8	792	96
a	**220.0000**	**0.0**	218.5144	−11.7	888	96
b♭	234.1371	7.8	232.5561	−3.9	996	108
b	247.5000	3.9	245.8281	−7.8	1092	96
c¹	263.4042	11.7	**261.6256**	**0.0**	1200	108

BEAT RATES

Note	5ths	4ths	M3rds	m3rds	M6ths
c	−1.3	0.0	1.5	−9.8	1.5
c#	0.0	0.0	8.7	−7.5	8.7
d	−1.5	2.0	4.2	−5.0	6.7
e♭	0.0	0.0	7.1	−11.6	9.8
e	0.0	0.0	7.5	−5.6	7.5
f	0.0	0.0	2.0	−13.0	5.0
f#	0.0	2.5	11.6	−10.0	11.6
g	−2.0	2.7	5.6	−10.6	5.6
g#	0.0	0.0	13.0	−11.2	13.0
a	0.0	3.0	10.0	−3.0	10.0
b♭	0.0	0.0	6.6	−17.3	10.6
b	−2.5	0.0	11.2	−13.4	11.2
c¹	−2.7	0.0	3.0	−19.5	3.0

Table 12.4. Kirnberger III

Note	A440 Frequency	A440 ET Dev.	A523.3 Frequency	A523.3 ET Dev.	Cumu- lative	Semi- tones
c	131.5906	10.3	**130.8128**	**0.0**	0	0
c#	138.6304	0.5	137.8109	−9.8	90	90
d	147.1228	3.4	146.2531	−6.8	193	103
e♭	155.9592	4.4	155.0373	−5.9	294	101
e	164.4884	−3.4	163.5160	−13.7	386	92
f	175.4541	8.3	174.4169	−2.0	498	112
f#	185.0494	0.5	183.9555	−9.8	590	92
g	196.7738	6.8	195.6107	−3.4	697	106
g#	207.9456	2.4	206.7163	−7.8	792	96
a	**220.0000**	**0.0**	218.6995	−10.3	890	98
b♭	233.9388	6.4	232.5559	−3.9	996	106
b	246.7325	−1.5	245.2740	−11.7	1088	92
c¹	263.1812	10.3	**261.6256**	**0.0**	1200	112

BEAT RATES

Note	5ths	4ths	M3rds	m3rds	M6ths
c	−1.2	0.0	0.0	−9.7	2.0
c#	0.0	0.6	8.7	−9.3	8.7
d	−1.4	1.8	4.6	−5.5	4.6
e♭	0.0	0.0	7.3	−10.5	9.7
e	0.0	2.0	9.3	−3.1	9.3
f	0.0	0.0	2.7	−13.0	5.5
f#	−0.6	0.0	10.5	−10.3	10.5
g	−1.8	2.4	3.1	−10.9	3.1
g#	0.0	0.0	13.0	−14.0	13.0
a	−2.0	2.7	9.0	−4.1	10.3
b♭	0.0	0.0	7.3	−17.3	10.9
b	0.0	0.0	14.0	−9.2	14.0
c¹	−2.4	0.0	0.0	−19.5	4.1

Table 12.5. Vallotti

Note	A440 Frequency	A440 ET Dev.	A523.3 Frequency	A523.3 ET Dev.	Cumulative	Semitones
c	131.2567	5.9	**130.8128**	**0.0**	0	0
c♯	138.5913	0.0	138.1226	−5.9	94	94
d	146.9983	2.0	146.5011	−3.9	196	102
e♭	155.9152	3.9	155.3879	−2.0	298	102
e	164.6278	−2.0	164.0710	−7.8	392	94
f	175.4046	7.8	174.8114	2.0	502	110
f♯	184.7884	−2.0	184.1635	−7.8	592	90
g	196.4409	3.9	195.7765	−2.0	698	106
g♯	207.8870	2.0	207.1839	−3.9	796	98
a	**220.0000**	**0.0**	219.2560	−5.9	894	98
b♭	233.8728	5.9	233.0819	0.0	1000	106
b	246.3846	−3.9	245.5513	−9.8	1090	90
c¹	262.5134	5.9	**261.6256**	**0.0**	1200	110

BEAT RATES

Note	5ths	4ths	M3rds	m3rds	M6ths
c	−0.9	1.2	2.2	−8.0	3.7
c♯	0.0	0.0	8.7	−8.4	8.7
d	−1.0	1.3	4.2	−5.0	4.2
e♭	0.0	0.0	6.2	−11.5	8.0
e	−1.1	1.5	8.4	−5.6	8.4
f	−1.2	0.0	3.0	−13.0	5.0
f♯	0.0	0.0	11.5	−8.7	11.5
g	−1.3	1.8	3.3	−9.3	5.6
g♯	0.0	0.0	10.6	−15.4	13.0
a	−1.5	2.0	8.7	−7.4	8.7
b♭	0.0	0.0	6.6	−17.3	9.3
b	0.0	2.2	15.4	−8.3	15.4
c¹	−1.8	2.4	4.5	−15.9	7.4

Table 12.6. Young No. 2

Note	A440 Frequency	A440 ET Dev.	A523.3 Frequency	A523.3 ET Dev.	Cumu- lative	Semi- tones
c	131.2567	5.9	**130.8128**	**0.0**	0	0
c♯	138.2787	-3.9	137.8110	-9.8	90	90
d	146.9983	2.0	146.5011	-3.9	196	106
e♭	155.5635	0.0	155.0374	-5.9	294	98
e	164.6278	-2.0	164.0710	-7.8	392	98
f	175.0089	3.9	174.4170	-2.0	498	106
f♯	184.3715	-5.9	183.7480	-11.7	588	90
g	196.4409	3.9	195.7765	-2.0	698	110
g♯	207.4180	-2.0	206.7165	-7.8	792	94
a	**220.0000**	**0.0**	219.2560	-5.9	894	102
b♭	233.3452	2.0	232.5561	-3.9	996	102
b	246.3846	-3.9	245.5513	-9.8	1090	94
c¹	262.5134	5.9	**261.6256**	**0.0**	1200	110

BEAT RATES

Note	5ths	4ths	M3rds	m3rds	M6ths
c	-0.9	0.0	2.2	-9.7	3.7
c♯	0.0	0.0	8.6	-6.5	8.6
d	-1.0	1.3	2.5	-6.9	4.2
e♭	0.0	0.0	7.9	-11.5	9.7
e	-1.1	1.5	6.5	-5.6	6.5
f	0.0	0.0	5.0	-13.0	6.9
f♯	0.0	1.7	11.5	-6.2	11.5
g	-1.3	1.8	3.3	-11.9	5.6
g♯	0.0	0.0	13.0	-12.6	13.0
a	-1.5	2.0	6.2	-7.4	6.2
b♭	0.0	0.0	9.3	-17.3	11.9
b	-1.7	2.2	12.6	-8.3	12.6
c¹	-1.8	0.0	4.5	-19.4	7.4

Table 12.7. Neidhardt Circulating Temperament No. 1

Note	A440 Frequency	A440 ET Dev.	A523.3 Frequency	A523.3 ET Dev.	Cumu- lative	Semi- tones
c	131.2567	5.9	**130.8128**	**0.0**	0	0
c#	138.5913	0.0	138.1226	−5.9	94	94
d	146.9983	2.0	146.5011	−3.9	196	102
e♭	155.7393	2.0	155.2125	−3.9	296	100
e	164.6278	−2.0	164.0710	−7.8	392	96
f	175.0089	3.9	174.4170	−2.0	498	106
f#	184.7884	−2.0	184.1635	−7.8	592	94
g	196.4409	3.9	195.7765	−2.0	698	106
g#	207.8870	2.0	207.1839	−3.9	796	98
a	**220.0000**	**0.0**	219.2560	−5.9	894	98
b♭	233.3452	2.0	232.5560	−3.9	996	102
b	246.6629	−2.0	245.8287	−7.8	1092	96
c¹	262.5134	5.9	**261.6256**	**0.0**	1200	108

BEAT RATES

Note	5ths	4ths	M3rds	m3rds	M6ths
c	−0.9	0.0	2.2	−8.8	3.7
c#	0.0	0.0	7.1	−8.4	7.1
d	−1.0	1.3	4.2	−6.9	5.0
e♭	−0.5	0.7	7.1	−10.5	8.8
e	−0.6	1.5	8.4	−5.6	8.4
f	0.0	0.0	5.0	−10.6	6.9
f#	0.0	0.8	9.4	−8.7	10.5
g	−1.3	1.8	4.4	−11.9	5.6
g#	−0.7	0.0	10.6	−14.0	10.6
a	−1.5	2.0	8.7	−7.4	8.7
b♭	0.0	1.1	9.3	−14.2	11.9
b	−0.8	1.1	12.6	−10.0	14.0
c¹	−1.8	0.0	4.5	−17.7	7.4

Table 12.8. *Tempérament Ordinaire*

Note	A440 Frequency	A440 ET Dev.	A523.3 Frequency	A523.3 ET Dev.	Cumu-lative	Semi-tones
c	131.4347	8.2	**130.8128**	**0.0**	0	0
c#	138.4662	−1.6	137.8110	−9.8	90	90
d	147.0647	2.7	146.3688	−5.5	195	104
e♭	155.7744	2.3	155.0374	−5.9	294	100
e	164.5534	−2.7	163.7748	−10.9	389	95
f	175.7218	10.9	174.8904	2.7	503	114
f#	184.6216	−3.5	183.7480	−11.7	588	86
g	196.6184	5.5	195.6881	−2.7	697	109
g#	207.6993	0.4	206.7165	−7.8	792	95
a	**220.0000**	**0.0**	218.9590	−8.2	892	100
b♭	233.9785	6.6	232.8714	−1.6	998	107
b	246.1621	−5.5	244.9973	−13.7	1086	88
c¹	262.8694	8.2	**261.6256**	**0.0**	1200	114

BEAT RATES

Note	5ths	4ths	M3rds	m3rds	M6ths
c	−1.1	1.4	1.0	−9.7	2.8
c#	0.0	0.0	10.6	−8.0	9.6
d	−1.2	1.6	3.2	−3.8	3.2
e♭	0.6	0.0	7.6	−11.5	9.7
e	−1.3	1.8	8.0	−4.2	8.0
f	−1.4	−1.0	1.4	−15.8	3.8
f#	0.0	0.0	12.8	−7.7	11.5
g	−1.6	2.1	1.6	−9.8	4.2
g#	0.0	0.0	13.0	−15.4	15.8
a	−1.8	2.4	7.7	−5.7	7.7
b♭	1.0	−1.3	6.6	−19.2	9.8
b	0.0	2.7	15.4	−6.3	15.4
c¹	−2.1	2.9	2.1	−19.5	5.7

Table 12.9. 1/6-Comma Meantone Temperament

Note	A440 Frequency	A440 ET Dev.	A523.3 Frequency	A523.3 ET Dev.	Cumu-lative	Semi-tones
c	131.1827	4.9	**130.8128**	**0.0**	0	0
c♯	138.0706	−6.5	137.6813	−11.4	89	89
d	146.9706	1.6	146.5563	−3.3	197	108
e♭	156.4444	9.8	156.0033	4.9	305	108
e	164.6587	−1.6	164.1945	−6.5	393	89
f	175.2727	6.5	174.7785	1.6	502	108
f♯	184.4756	−4.9	183.9555	−9.8	590	89
g	196.3670	3.3	195.8133	−1.6	698	108
g♯	206.6775	−8.1	206.0947	−13.0	787	89
a	**220.0000**	**0.0**	219.3797	−4.9	895	108
b♭	234.1813	8.1	233.5210	3.3	1003	108
b	246.4773	−3.3	245.7823	−8.1	1092	89
c^l	262.3653	4.9	**261.6256**	**0.0**	1200	108

BEAT RATES

Note	5ths	4ths	M3rds	m3rds	M6ths
c	−0.8	1.1	2.7	−4.9	4.1
c♯	−0.9	1.1	10.7	−5.1	12.2
d	−0.9	1.2	3.0	−5.5	4.6
e♭	−1.0	−5.7	3.2	−16.3	4.9
e	−1.0	1.4	3.4	−6.1	5.1
f	−1.1	1.5	3.6	−18.2	5.5
f♯	−1.1	1.5	14.3	−6.9	16.3
g	−1.2	1.6	4.1	−7.3	6.1
g♯	5.7	1.7	16.1	−7.7	18.2
a	−1.4	1.8	4.6	−8.2	6.9
b♭	−1.5	1.9	4.9	−24.4	7.3
b	−1.5	2.0	19.2	−9.2	7.7
c^l	−1.6	2.2	5.4	−9.7	8.2

Table 12.10. Rameau

Note	A440 Frequency	A440 ET Dev.	A523.3 Frequency	A523.3 ET Dev.	Cumu- lative	Semi- tones
c	131.5907	10.3	**130.8128**	**0.0**	0	0
c#	138.3567	−2.9	137.5388	−13.2	87	87
d	147.1229	3.4	146.2531	−6.8	193	106
eb	156.2899	8.1	155.3659	−2.2	298	105
e	164.4884	−3.4	163.5160	−13.7	386	89
f	176.0000	13.7	174.9596	−3.4	503	117
f#	184.4756	−4.9	183.3851	−15.2	585	81
g	196.7740	6.8	195.6107	−3.4	697	112
g#	207.5351	−1.0	206.3082	−11.2	789	92
a	**220.0000**	**0.0**	218.6995	−10.3	890	101
bb	235.3966	17.1	234.0050	6.8	1007	117
b	245.9675	−6.8	244.5134	−17.1	1083	76
c^l	263.1814	10.3	**261.6256**	**0.0**	1200	117

BEAT RATES

Note	5ths	4ths	M3rds	m3rds	M6ths
c	−1.2	1.6	0	−8.1	2.0
c#	0.0	0.0	12.2	−7.7	14.4
d	−1.4	1.8	2.3	−2.7	2.3
eb	1.9	−2.6	5.6	−15.4	8.1
e	−1.5	2.0	7.7	−3.1	7.7
f	−1.6	2.2	0	−18.3	2.7
f#	0.0	0.0	19.2	−6.9	15.4
g	−1.8	2.4	0	−3.7	3.1
g#	2.6	0.0	15.1	−15.4	18.3
a	−2.0	2.7	6.9	−4.1	6.9
bb	−2.2	−3.8	0	−28.8	3.7
b	0.0	3.1	20.5	−4.6	15.4
c^l	−2.4	3.3	0	−16.2	4.1

Table 12.11. Sorge

Note	A440 Frequency	A440 ET Dev.	A523.3 Frequency	A523.3 ET Dev.	Cumu-lative	Semi-tones
c	131.2567	5.9	**130.8128**	**0.0**	0	0
c♯	138.5913	0.0	138.1226	−5.9	94	94
d	146.9983	2.0	146.5011	−3.9	196	102
e♭	155.9152	3.9	155.3879	2.0	298	102
e	165.0000	2.0	164.4420	−3.9	396	98
f	175.0089	3.9	174.4170	−2.0	498	102
f♯	184.9972	0.0	184.3715	−5.9	594	96
g	196.4409	3.9	195.7765	−2.0	698	104
g♯	207.8870	2.0	207.1839	−3.9	796	98
a	**220.0000**	**0.0**	219.2560	−5.9	894	98
b♭	233.6089	3.9	232.8188	−2.0	998	104
b	246.9417	0.0	246.1065	−3.9	1094	96
c¹	262.5134	5.9	**261.6256**	**0.0**	1200	106

BEAT RATES

Note	5ths	4ths	M3rds	m3rds	M6ths
c	−0.9	0.0	3.7	−8.0	3.7
c♯	0.0	0.6	7.1	−6.5	7.9
d	−1.0	1.3	5.0	−6.9	5.8
e♭	−0.5	0.0	6.2	−10.5	8.0
e	−1.1	0.0	6.5	−7.8	6.5
f	0.0	0.8	5.0	−10.6	6.9
f♯	−0.6	0.8	9.4	−10.0	10.5
g	−1.3	1.8	5.6	−10.6	7.8
g♯	0.0	0.0	10.6	−12.6	10.6
a	0.0	2.0	8.7	−7.4	10.0
b♭	−0.8	1.1	7.9	−15.7	10.6
b	−0.8	2.2	12.6	−11.7	12.6
c¹	−1.8	0.0	7.4	−15.9	7.4

Table 12.12. Young No. 1

Note	A440 Frequency	A440 ET Dev.	A523.3 Frequency	A523.3 ET Dev.	Cumulative	Semitones
c	131.2567	5.9	**130.8128**	**0.0**	0	0
c#	138.5913	0.0	138.1226	−5.9	94	94
d	146.9983	2.0	146.5011	−3.9	196	102
eb	155.9152	3.9	155.3879	−2.0	298	102
e	164.6278	−2.0	164.0710	−7.8	392	94
f	175.2067	5.9	174.6141	0.0	500	108
f#	184.7884	−2.0	184.1635	−7.8	592	92
g	196.4409	3.9	195.7765	−2.0	698	106
g#	207.8870	2.0	207.1839	−3.9	796	98
a	**220.0000**	**0.0**	219.2560	−5.9	894	98
bb	233.8728	5.9	233.0819	0.0	1000	106
b	246.6629	−2.0	245.8287	−7.8	1092	92
c¹	262.5134	5.9	**261.6256**	**0.0**	1200	108

BEAT RATES

Note	5ths	4ths	M3rds	m3rds	M6ths
c	−0.9	0.6	2.2	−8.0	3.7
c#	0.0	0.0	7.9	−8.4	8.7
d	−1.0	1.3	4.2	−6.0	5.0
eb	0.0	0.0	6.2	−11.5	8.0
e	−0.6	1.5	8.4	−5.6	8.4
f	−0.6	0.8	4.0	−11.8	6.0
f#	0.0	0.8	11.5	−8.7	11.5
g	−1.3	1.8	4.4	−9.3	5.6
g#	0.0	0.0	10.6	−14.0	11.8
a	−1.5	2.0	8.7	−7.4	8.7
bb	−0.8	0.0	6.6	−17.3	9.3
b	−0.8	1.1	14.0	−10.0	14.0
c¹	−1.8	1.2	4.5	−15.9	7.4

Table 12.13. Kellner

Note	A440 Frequency	A440 ET Dev.	A523.3 Frequency	A523.3 ET Dev.	Cumu-lative	Semi-tones
c	131.4347	8.2	**130.8128**	**0.0**	0	0
c♯	138.4662	−1.6	137.8110	−9.8	90	90
d	147.0647	2.7	146.3688	−5.5	195	104
e♭	155.7744	2.3	155.0374	−5.9	294	100
e	164.5534	−2.7	163.7748	−10.9	389	95
f	175.2462	6.3	174.4170	−2.0	498	109
f♯	184.6216	−3.5	183.7480	−11.7	588	90
g	196.6184	5.5	195.6881	−2.7	697	109
g♯	207.6993	0.4	206.7165	−7.8	792	95
a	**220.0000**	**0.0**	218.9590	−8.2	892	100
b♭	233.6617	4.3	232.5561	−3.9	996	104
b	246.8301	−0.8	245.6622	9.0	1091	95
c^l	262.8694	8.2	**261.6256**	**0.0**	1200	109

BEAT RATES

Note	5ths	4ths	M3rds	m3rds	M6ths
c	−1.1	0.0	1.0	−9.7	2.8
c♯	0.0	0.0	8.7	−8.0	8.7
d	−1.2	1.6	3.2	−6.2	5.2
e♭	0.0	0.0	7.6	−11.5	9.7
e	0.0	1.8	8.0	−4.2	8.0
f	0.0	0.0	3.8	−13.0	6.2
f♯	0.0	2.0	11.5	−7.7	11.5
g	−1.6	2.1	4.2	−11.4	4.2
g♯	0.0	0.0	13.0	−12.0	13.0
a	−1.8	2.4	7.7	−5.7	7.7
b♭	0.0	0.0	8.2	−17.3	11.4
b	−2.0	0.0	12.0	−10.3	12.0
c^l	−2.1	0.0	2.1	−19.5	5.7

Table 12.14. Barnes

Note	A440 Frequency	A440 ET Dev.	A523.3 Frequency	A523.3 ET Dev.	Cumu- lative	Semi- tones
c	131.2567	5.9	**130.8128**	**0.0**	0	0
c#	138.5913	0.0	138.1226	−5.9	94	94
d	146.9983	2.0	146.5011	−3.9	196	102
e♭	155.9152	3.9	155.3879	−2.0	298	102
e	164.6278	−2.0	164.0710	−7.8	392	94
f	175.4046	7.8	174.8114	2.0	502	110
f#	184.7884	−2.0	184.1635	−7.8	592	90
g	196.4409	3.9	195.7765	−2.0	698	106
g#	207.8870	2.0	207.1839	−3.9	796	98
a	**220.0000**	**0.0**	219.2560	−5.9	894	98
b♭	233.8728	5.9	233.0819	0.0	1000	106
b	246.9417	0.0	246.1065	−5.9	1094	94
c¹	262.5134	5.9	**261.6256**	**0.0**	1200	106

BEAT RATES

Note	5ths	4ths	M3rds	m3rds	M6ths
c	−0.9	1.2	2.2	−8.0	3.7
c#	0.0	0.0	8.7	−8.4	8.7
d	−1.0	1.3	4.2	−5.0	5.8
e♭	0.0	0.0	6.2	−11.5	8.0
e	0.0	1.5	8.4	−5.6	8.4
f	−1.2	0.0	3.0	−13.0	5.0
f#	0.0	1.7	11.5	−8.7	11.5
g	−1.3	1.8	5.6	−9.3	5.6
g#	0.0	0.0	10.6	−12.6	13.0
a	−1.5	2.0	8.7	−7.4	8.7
b♭	0.0	0.0	6.6	−17.3	9.3
b	−1.7	0.0	12.6	−11.7	12.6
c¹	−1.8	2.4	4.5	−15.9	7.4

Table 12.15. Lindley

Note	A440 Frequency	A440 ET Dev.	A523.3 Frequency	A523.3 ET Dev.	Cumu- lative	Semi- tones
c	131.2567	5.9	**130.8128**	**0.0**	0	0
c♯	138.4349	−2.0	137.9667	−7.8	92	92
d	146.9983	2.0	146.5011	−3.9	196	104
e♭	155.7393	2.0	155.2125	−3.9	296	100
e	164.6278	−2.0	164.0710	−7.8	392	96
f	175.2067	5.9	174.6141	0.0	500	108
f♯	184.5799	−3.9	183.9556	−9.8	590	90
g	196.4409	3.9	195.7765	−2.0	698	108
g♯	207.6523	0.0	206.9501	−5.9	794	96
a	**220.0000**	**0.0**	219.2560	−5.9	894	100
b♭	233.6089	3.9	232.8188	−2.0	998	104
b	246.3846	−3.9	245.5513	−9.8	1090	92
c¹	262.5134	5.9	**261.6256**	**0.0**	1200	110

BEAT RATES

Note	5ths	4ths	M3rds	m3rds	M6ths
c	−0.9	0.6	2.2	−8.8	3.7
c♯	0.0	0.0	8.7	−7.5	8.7
d	−1.0	1.3	3.3	−6.0	4.2
e♭	0.0	0.0	7.1	−11.5	8.8
e	−1.1	1.5	7.5	−5.6	7.5
f	−0.6	0.0	4.0	−13.0	6.0
f♯	0.0	0.8	11.5	−7.5	11.5
g	−1.3	1.8	3.3	−10.6	5.6
g♯	0.0	0.0	11.8	−14.0	13.0
a	−1.5	2.0	7.5	−7.4	7.5
b♭	0.0	0.0	7.9	−17.3	10.6
b	−0.8	2.2	14.0	−8.3	14.0
c¹	−1.8	1.2	4.5	−17.7	7.4

Table 12.16. Equal Temperament

Note	A440 Frequency	A440 ET Dev.	A523.3 Frequency	A523.3 ET Dev.	Cumu- lative	Semi- tones
c	130.8128	0	**130.8128**	**0**	0	0
c#	138.5913	0	138.5913	0	100	100
d	146.8324	0	146.8324	0	200	100
eb	155.5635	0	155.5635	0	300	100
e	164.8138	0	164.8138	0	400	100
f	174.6141	0	174.6141	0	500	100
f#	184.9972	0	184.9972	0	600	100
g	195.9977	0	195.9977	0	700	100
g#	207.6523	0	207.6523	0	800	100
a	**220.0000**	**0**	220.0000	0	900	100
bb	233.0819	0	233.0819	0	1000	100
b	246.9417	0	246.9417	0	1100	100
c¹	261.6256	0	**261.6256**	**0**	1200	100

BEAT RATES

Note	5ths	4ths	M3rds	m3rds	M6ths
c	−0.4	0.6	5.2	−7.1	5.9
c#	−0.5	0.6	5.5	−7.5	6.3
d	−0.5	0.7	5.8	−7.9	6.7
eb	−0.5	0.7	6.2	−8.4	7.1
e	−0.6	0.7	6.5	−8.9	7.5
f	−0.6	0.8	6.9	−9.4	7.9
f#	−0.6	0.8	7.3	−10.0	8.4
g	−0.7	0.9	7.8	−10.6	8.9
g#	−0.7	0.9	8.2	−11.2	9.4
a	−0.7	1.0	8.7	−11.9	10.0
bb	−0.8	1.1	9.2	−12.6	10.6
b	−0.8	1.1	9.8	−13.3	11.2
c¹	−0.9	1.2	10.4	−14.1	11.9

Table 12.17. Near-Equal Temperament

Note	A440 Frequency	A440 ET Dev.	A523.3 Frequency	A523.3 ET Dev.	Cumu- lative	Semi- tones
c	130.6651	−2.0	**130.8128**	0.0	0	0
c#	138.5913	0.0	138.7479	2.0	102	102
d	146.6667	−2.0	146.8324	0.0	200	98
e♭	155.5635	0.0	155.7393	2.0	302	102
e	164.6278	−2.0	164.8138	0.0	400	98
f	174.6141	0.0	174.8114	2.0	502	102
f#	184.7884	−2.0	184.9972	0.0	600	98
g	195.9977	0.0	196.2192	2.0	702	102
g#	207.4180	−2.0	207.6524	0.0	800	98
a	**220.0000**	**0.0**	220.2486	2.0	902	102
b♭	232.8188	−2.0	233.0819	0.0	1000	98
b	246.9417	0.0	247.2207	2.0	1102	102
c¹	261.3303	−2.0	**261.6256**	0.0	1200	98

BEAT RATES

Note	5ths	4ths	M3rds	m3rds	M6ths
c	0.0	1.2	5.2	−6.2	6.7
c#	−0.9	0.0	5.5	−8.4	5.5
d	0.0	1.3	5.8	−6.9	7.5
e♭	−1.1	0.0	6.2	−9.4	6.2
e	0.0	1.5	6.5	−7.8	8.4
f	−1.2	0.0	6.9	−10.6	6.9
f#	0.0	1.7	7.3	−8.7	9.4
g	−1.3	0.0	7.8	−11.9	7.8
g#	0.0	1.9	8.2	−9.8	10.6
a	−1.5	0.0	8.7	−13.3	8.7
b♭	0.0	2.1	9.2	−11.0	11.9
b	−1.7	0.0	9.8	−15.0	9.8
c¹	0.0	2.4	10.4	−12.3	13.3

Ensemble Considerations

There are often discussions about the compatibility of a keyboard temperament with other instruments when playing in ensemble. Since most instruments have the capability of flexible intonation, it is possible for most instruments to alter intonation to blend with a fixed-intonation keyboard instrument. The one inflexible aspect of ensemble playing is the open strings of the bowed stringed instruments: violin (g, d^l, a^l, e^2), viola (c, g, d^l, a^l), and cello (C, G, d, a). Table 12.18 presents data with respect to the beat rates between selected temperaments and these open strings. The beat rates are not derived from coinciding harmonic frequencies, but from unison pitches. The pitch reference is a^l = A440, so the beat rates for a and a^l are all zero. A negative sign means the note is lower in the keyboard temperament compared to the strings.

It is assumed that all open strings of the bowed instruments are tuned to pure fifths. This does not necessarily have to be so; it is entirely possible to tune open strings as narrow fifths.[1]

The most problematic note is the top string of the violin in relation to all temperaments except Werckmeister III and Sorge. The situation of most concern would be the simultaneous sounding of the e^2 string with the same note on a continuo organ. The decay of a vibrating string may make this less of a problem with the harpsichord. Also, it should be remembered that slightly out-of-tune unisons produces a chorus effect, which is not necessarily an undesirable quality.

Table 12.18. Beat Rates of Selected Temperaments Compared to the Open Strings of Bowed Stringed Instruments (Violin, Viola, Cello)

Name	C	G	c	d	g	a	d^l	a^l	e^2
1/4-comma meantone,									
Kirnberger III	0.6	0.6	1.2	0.5	1.2	0	0.9	0	−2.1
Werckmeister III	0.7	0.7	1.3	0.5	1.3	0	1.0	0	0
Vallotti[a]	0.4	0.4	0.9	0.3	0.9	0	0.7	0	−1.5
Neidhardt	0.5	0.5	0.9	0.4	0.9	0	0.7	0	−1.5
ordinaire	0.6	0.6	1.1	0.4	1.1	0	0.9	0	−1.9
1/6-comma meantone	0.4	0.4	0.8	0.3	0.8	0	0.6	0	−1.4
Rameau	0.6	0.6	1.2	0.5	1.2	0	0.9	0	−2.0
Sorge	0.6	0.6	1.1	0.6	1.2	0	1.2	0	0
Kellner	0.5	0.5	1.1	0.4	1.1	0	0.8	0	−1.8
equal	0.2	0.2	0.4	0.2	0.4	0	0.3	0	−0.7
near equal	0.1	0.2	0.3	0	0.4	0	0	0	−1.5

a. also Young no. 1, Young no. 2, Barnes, and Lindley

Note

1. Bruce Haynes, "Beyond Temperament: Non-Keyboard Intonation in the 17th and 18th Centuries," *Early Music* 19 (August 1991): 359.

13

Temperament Spreadsheets

The description of fifths in a temperament may be presented in terms of a shorthand notation (−1/6 PC, −1/12 PC), cent values (696 cents, 700 cents), or comma distribution (−4 cents, −2 cents). This was discussed in chapter 2. Occasionally one sees a temperament described in two other ways. First, each note is given a value that represents its frequency's deviation in cents from the corresponding equal temperament frequency. The result is a series of numbers such as

$$6, 0, 2, 1, \quad 2, 8, \quad 2, 1, 2, 0, 6, \quad 1, 6.$$

This method is found, for example, in *Tuning* by Owen Jorgensen.[1] Second, each note is given a number which is the cumulative sum of the semitones in cents; that is, any given C is 0 cents, the C an octave higher is 1200 cents, and the cumulative sum results in a series of numbers such as

$$0, 94, 196, 298, 392, 502, 592, 698, 796, 894, 1000, 1090, 1200.$$

This method is found in *Tuning and Temperament* by J. Murray Barbour.[2] While each approach can correctly describe a temperament in its own way, they do not offer an immediate sense of the tempering of the fifths, and they are based on a chromatic sequence of notes (C, C♯, D, E♭, and so on), not the circle of fifths (C, G, D, A, and so on). It takes considerable experience and practice if one is to determine that the two sequences given above represent the Vallotti temperament.

The purpose of this chapter is to present computer spreadsheets that may be used to convert alternate temperament expressions such as cent deviations and cumulative semitone values into frequencies, beat rates, and sizes of fifths and major thirds. An additional spreadsheet will also be included in which the comma distribution of a temperament may also be used as an input. The original format for the spreadsheet was done on Microsoft® Excel 2002.

The three spreadsheets are entitled "Cent Deviations," "Cumulative Semitones," and "Comma Distribution." They are shown in Figures 13.1, 13.2, and 13.3 at the end of the chapter. The cent deviations spreadsheet will be described in detail, and then the modifications to it to create the other two will be discussed. Each spreadsheet is divided in three sections: section I includes rows 1 to 17; section II includes rows 19 to 33; and section III includes rows 35 to 49. Each section has both labeling and formulas.

While entering the items, be sure to select a file name and save your work periodically.

Spreadsheet No. 1: Cent Deviations

Section I Labeling

A1: "Name:"	E4: "from E.T."	A9: "*e*"
E1: "Cent Deviations"	F3: "Cumulative"	A10: "*f*"
A4: "Note"	F4: "Semitones"	A11: "*f#*"
B3: "Equal Temp."	G3: "Individual"	A12: "*g*"
B4: "Frequency"	G4: "Semitones"	A13: "*g#*"
C3: "***Variable:***"	A5: "*c*"	A14: "*a*"
C4: "***Cent Dev.***"	A6: "*c#*"	A15: "*bb*"
D4: "Frequency"	A7: "*d*"	A16: "*b*"
E3: "Cent Dev."	A8: "*eb*"	A17: "*c1*"

(Procedure note: Type the text inside the quotation marks, not the quotation marks themselves. The text in cell E1 will extend into cell F1. Cells C3 and C4 are in bold italic type to denote where input data will be placed. Cells A5 to A17 are in lowercase italic type to denote actual pitches in the tenor octave. For simplicity, the pound sign is used in place of the sharp sign, and a lowercase B is used for the flat sign.)

Section I Formulas

Cells B5 to B17 contain the equal temperament frequencies for the tenor-octave notes c to c^1. The rationale is to use 220 Hz for the reference pitch for a, then calculate the other frequencies based on the fact that each adjacent semitone is related to its neighbor by the *twelfth root of two*, or its equivalent expression *two to the one-twelfth power* ($2^{1/12}$). Each note below a is calculated by dividing its higher neighbor by $2^{1/12}$, while each note above a is calculated by multiplying its lower neighbor by $2^{1/12}$.

B5: =B6/(2^(1/12))
B6: =B7/(2^(1/12))
B7: =B8/(2^(1/12))
B8: =B9/(2^(1/12))
B9: =B10/(2^(1/12))
B10: =B11/(2^(1/12))
B11: =B12/(2^(1/12))

B12: =B13/(2^(1/12))
B13: =B14/(2^(1/12))
B14: 220
B15: –B14*(2^(1/12))
B16: =B15*(2^(1/12))
B17: =B16*(2^(1/12))

(Procedure note: Type the given formula in cell B5, then copy and paste to cells B6 through B13. Type the value of 220 in cell B14. Type the given formula in cell B15, then copy and paste to cells B16 and B17.)

Cells C5 to C17 are left blank. These are the cells into which one inserts the given values for the cent deviations from equal temperament.

Cells D5 to D17 are the frequencies of the temperament in question. These frequencies are calculated using the rearranged cent equation, the equal temperament frequencies in cells B5 to B17, and the cent values inserted in cells C5 to C17.

D5: =B5*(10^(C5/3986.3137))
D6: =B6*(10^(C6/3986.3137))
D7: =B7*(10^(C7/3986.3137))
D8: =B8*(10^(C8/3986.3137))
D9: =B9*(10^(C9/3986.3137))
D10: =B10*(10^(C10/3986.3137))
D11: =B11*(10^(C11/3986.3137))

D12: =B12*(10^(C12/3986.3137))
D13: =B13*(10^(C13/3986.3137))
D14: =B14*(10^(C14/3986.3137))
D15: =B15*(10^(C15/3986.3137))
D16: =B16*(10^(C16/3986.3137))
D17: =B17*(10^(C17/3986.3137))

(Procedure note: Type the given formula in cell D5, then copy and paste to cells D6 through D17.)

Cells E5 to E17 contain the cent deviation of the selected temperament's frequencies compared to equal temperament. This is redundant for this particular spreadsheet, but is included so it may be calculated for the other two spreadsheets. The cent deviation is calculated using the regular form of the cent equation.

E5: =3986.3137*LOG(D5/B5)   E12: =3986.3137*LOG(D12/B12)
E6: =3986.3137*LOG(D6/B6)   E13: =3986.3137*LOG(D13/B13)
E7: =3986.3137*LOG(D7/B7)   E14: =3986.3137*LOG(D14/B14)
E8: =3986.3137*LOG(D8/B8)   E15: =3986.3137*LOG(D15/B15)
E9: =3986.3137*LOG(D9/B9)   E16: =3986.3137*LOG(D16/B16)
E10: =3986.3137*LOG(D10/B10)   E17: =3986.3137*LOG(D17/B17)
E11: =3986.3137*LOG(D11/B11)

(Procedure note: Type the given formula in cell E5, then copy and paste to cells E6 through E17.)

Cells F5 to F17 give the cumulative semitones. These are calculated using the cent equation with a minor modification: each frequency from the selected temperament is compared to the frequency of *c*; that is, the lower value in the frequency ratio for all the formulas is D5.

F5: 0   F12: =3986.3137*LOG(D12/D5)
F6: =3986.3137*LOG(D6/D5)   F13: =3986.3137*LOG(D13/D5)
F7: =3986.3137*LOG(D7/D5)   F14: =3986.3137*LOG(D14/D5)
F8: =3986.3137*LOG(D8/D5)   F15: =3986.3137*LOG(D15/D5)
F9: =3986.3137*LOG(D9/D5)   F16: =3986.3137*LOG(D16/D5)
F10: =3986.3137*LOG(D10/D5)   F17: =3986.3137*LOG(D17/D5)
F11: =3986.3137*LOG(D11/D5)

(Procedure note: Type the given formula in cell F6, copy and paste to cells F7 through F17, then change the last term in cells F7 through F17 to "D5".)

Cells G5 to G17 give the individual semitones. These are read as follows: each value is the size of the semitone for the given note and its *lower* neighbor; that is, if the value in cell G6 is 94, this is the *c♯* row, but it represents the size of the *c–c♯* semitone. These are calculated by simple subtraction of the values in the F column.

G5: 0
G6: =F6
G7: =F7-F6
G8: =F8-F7
G9: =F9-F8
G10: =F10-F9
G11: =F11-F10

G12: =F12-F11
G13: =F13-F12
G14: =F14-F13
G15: =F15-F14
G16: =F16-F15
G17: =F17-F16

(Procedure note: Type the given formula in cell G7, then copy and paste to cells G8 through G17.)

Section II Labeling

B19: "Beat Rates"
A20: "Note"
B20: "5th"
C20: "4th"
D20: "M3rd"
E20: "m3rd"
F20: "M6th"

A21: "*c*"
A22: "*c#*"
A23: "*d*"
A24: "*eb*"
A25: "*e*"
A26: "*f*"
A27: "*f#*"

A28: "*g*"
A29: "*g#*"
A30: "*a*"
A31: "*bb*"
A32: "*b*"
A33: "*c1*"

(Procedure note: The items in cells A21 through A33 may be copied and pasted from cells A5 through A17.)

Section II Formulas

These formulas are based on the method of beat calculation presented in chapter 4.

B21: =(D12*2)-(D5*3)
B22: =(D13*2)-(D6*3)
B23: =(D14*2)-(D7*3)
B24: =(D15*2)-(D8*3)
B25: =(D16*2)-(D9*3)
B26: =(D17*2)-(D10*3)
B27: =((D6*2)*2)-(D11*3)

B28: =((D7*2)*2)-(D12*3)
B29: =((D8*2)*2)-(D13*3)
B30: =((D9*2)*2)-(D14*3)
B31: =((D10*2)*2)-(D15*3)
B32: =((D11*2)*2)-(D16*3)
B33: =((D12*2)*2)-(D17*3)

(Procedure note: Type the given formula in cell B21, then copy and paste to cells B22 through B26. Type the given formula in cell B27, then copy and paste to cells B28 through B33.)

C21: =(D10*3)-(D5*4)   C28: =(D17*3)-(D12*4)
C22: =(D11*3)-(D6*4)   C29: =((D6*2)*3)-(D13*4)
C23: =(D12*3)-(D7*4)   C30: =((D7*2)*3)-(D14*4)
C24: =(D13*3)-(D8*4)   C31: =((D8*2)*3)-(D15*4)
C25: =(D14*3)-(D9*4)   C32: =((D9*2)*3)-(D16*4)
C26: =(D15*3)-(D10*4)   C33: =((D10*2)*3)-(D17*4)
C27: =(D16*3)-(D11*4)

(Procedure note: Type the given formula in cell C21, then copy and paste to cells C22 through C28. Type the given formula in cell C29, then copy and paste to cells C30 through C33.)

D21: =(D9*4)-(D5*5)   D28: =(D16*4)-(D12*5)
D22: =(D10*4)-(D6*5)   D29: =(D17*4)-(D13*5)
D23: =(D11*4)-(D7*5)   D30: =((D6*2)*4)-(D14*5)
D24: =(D12*4)-(D8*5)   D31: =((D7*2)*4)-(D15*5)
D25: =(D13*4)-(D9*5)   D32: =((D8*2)*4)-(D16*5)
D26: =(D14*4)-(D10*5)   D33: =((D9*2)*4)-(D17*5)
D27: =(D15*4)-(D11*5)

(Procedure note: Type the given formula in cell D21, then copy and paste to cells D22 through D29. Type the given formula in cell D30, then copy and paste to cells D31 through D33.)

E21: =(D8*5)-(D5*6)   E28: =(D15*5)-(D12*6)
E22: =(D9*5)-(D6*6)   E29: =(D16*5)-(D13*6)
E23: =(D10*5)-(D7*6)   E30: =(D17*5)-(D14*6)
E24: =(D11*5)-(D8*6)   E31: =((D6*2)*5)-(D15*6)
E25: =(D12*5)-(D9*6)   E32: =((D7*2)*5)-(D16*6)
E26: =(D13*5)-(D10*6)   E33: =((D8*2)*5)-(D17*6)
E27: =(D14*5)-(D11*6)

(Procedure note: Type the given formula in cell E21, then copy and paste to cells E22 through E30. Type the given formula in cell E31, then copy and paste to cells E32 and E33.)

F21: =(D14*3)-(D5*5)   F28: =((D9*2)*3)-(D12*5)
F22: =(D15*3)-(D6*5)   F29: =((D10*2)*3)-(D13*5)
F23: =(D16*3)-(D7*5)   F30: =((D11*2)*3)-(D14*5)
F24: =(D17*3)-(D8*5)   F31: =((D12*2)*3)-(D15*5)

F25: =((D6*2)*3)-(D9*5)   F32: =((D13*2)*3)-(D16*5)
F26: =((D7*2)*3)-(D10*5)   F33: =((D14*2)*3)-(D17*5)
F27: =((D8*2)*3)-(D11*5)

(Procedure note: Type the given formula in cell F21, then copy and paste to cells F22 through F24. Type the given formula in cell F25, then copy and paste to cells F26 through F33.)

Section III Labeling

A35: "5th"	A37: "C-G"	E37: "C-E"
A36: "Interval"	A38: "G-D"	E38: "G-B"
B35: "5th"	A39: "D-A"	E39: "D-F#"
B36: "Cents"	A40: "A-E"	E40: "A-C#"
C35: "5th"	A41: "E-B"	E41: "E-G#"
C36: "Comma"	A42: "B-F#"	E42: "B-Eb"
E35: "M3rd"	A43: "F#-C#"	E43: "F#-Bb"
E36: "Interval"	A44: "C#-G#"	E44: "C#-F"
F35: "M3rds"	A45: "G#-Eb"	E45: "G#-C"
F36: "Cents"	A46: "Eb-Bb"	E46: "Eb-G"
G35: "M3rds"	A47: "Bb-F"	E47: "Bb-D"
G36: "Comma"	A48: "F-C"	E48: "F-A"

Section III Formulas

B37: =3986.3137*LOG(D12/D5)
B38: =3986.3137*LOG((D7*2)/D12)
B39: =3986.3137*LOG(D14/D7)
B40: =3986.3137*LOG((D9*2)/D14)
B41: =3986.3137*LOG(D16/D9)
B42: =3986.3137*LOG((D11*2)/D16)
B43: =3986.3137*LOG((D6*2)/D11)
B44: =3986.3137*LOG(D13/D6)
B45: =3986.3137*LOG((D8*2)/D13)
B46: =3986.3137*LOG(D15/D8)
B47: =3986.3137*LOG((D10*2/D15)
B48: =3986.3137*LOG(D17/D10)
B49: = SUM(B37:B48)

(Procedure note: Use italics for cell B49.)

C37: =B37-702   C44: =B44-702
C38: =B38-702   C45: =B45-702
C39: =B39-702   C46: =B46-702
C40: =B40-702   C47: =B47-702
C41: =B41-702   C48: =B48-702
C42: =B42-702   C49: =SUM(C37:C48)
C43: =B43-702

(Procedure notes: Type the given formula in cell C37, then copy and paste to cells C38 through C48. Cell C49 may be copied from B49, and is in italics.)

F37: =3986.3137*LOG(D9/D5)
F38: =3986.3137*LOG(D16/D12)
F39: =3986.3137*LOG(D11/D7)
F40: =3986.3137*LOG((D6*2)/D14)
F41: =3986.3137*LOG(D13/D9)
F42: =3986.3137*LOG((D8*2)/D16)
F43: =3986.3137*LOG(D15/D11)
F44: =3986.3137*LOG(D10/D6)
F45: =3986.3137*LOG(D17/D13)
F46: =3986.3137*LOG(D12/D8)
F47: =3986.3137*LOG((D7*2/D15)
F48: =3986.3137*LOG(D14/D10)
F49: =SUM(F37:F48)

(Procedure note: Cell F49 may be copied from B49 and is in italics.)

G37: =F37-386   G41: =F41-386   G45: =F45-386
G38: =F38-386   G42: =F42-386   G46: =F46-386
G39: =F39-386   G43: =F43-386   G47: =F47-386
G40: =F40-386   G44: =F44-386   G48: =F48-386

(Procedure note: Type the given formula in cell G37, then copy and paste to cells G38 through G48.)

Once the spreadsheet is completed, the widths of columns A through G are adjusted. Click on the "A" at the top of column A to highlight the entire column, hold down the Shift key, and use the right arrow key (→) to highlight columns A through G. Right-click within the highlighted area, click on "Column Width," and type in the value of 10. Click "OK."

Certain sets of numbers in the spreadsheet are set to different decimal places (table 13.1).

Table 13.1. Decimal Places for the Spreadsheets

Cells	Decimal Places	Example
B5 to B17	4	195.9977
D5 to D17	4	196.4511
E5 to E17	0 or 1	4 or 3.9
F5 to F17	0	698
G5 to G17	0	106
B21 to B33,		
C21 to C33,		
D21 to D33,		
E21 to E33, and		
F21 to F33	1	−1.3
B37 to B48	0	698
C37 to C48	0 or 1	−4 or −4.0
F37 to F48	0	392
G37 to G48	0	6

The decimal places are set by highlighting certain cells and clicking on the "Decrease Decimal" icon. Sometimes one cannot adjust the decimal places of all twelve or thirteen numbers in the set at the same time, in which case they need to be done separately. This is due to the fact that some of the numbers are not computed by formulas but are actual numbers, such as "220" in cell B14 and "0" in cells F5 and G5.

Spreadsheet No. 2: Cumulative Semitones

Spreadsheet no. 1, cent deviations, is copied in its entirety and pasted into a second worksheet. The widths of columns A through G will again need to be set at 10. Spreadsheet no. 2, cumulative semitones, is the same as spreadsheet no. 1 except for the following changes.

Section I Labeling

E1: "Cumulative Semitones"
C4: *"Cumul. ST"*

Section I Formulas

D5: =220/(10^((C14-C5)/3986.3137))
D6: =220/(10^((C14-C6)/3986.3137))
D7: =220/(10^((C14-C7)/3986.3137))
D8: =220/(10^((C14-C8)/3986.3137))
D9: =220/(10^((C14-C9)/3986.3137))
D10: =220/(10^((C14-C10)/3986.3137))
D11: =220/(10^((C14-C11)/3986.3137))
D12: =220/(10^((C14-C12)/3986.3137))
D13: =220/(10^((C14-C13)/3986.3137))
D14: =220
D15: =220*(10^((C15-C14)/3986.3137))
D16: =220*(10^((C16-C14)/3986.3137))
D17: =220*(10^((C17-C14)/3986.3137))

Spreadsheet No. 3: Comma Distribution

Spreadsheet no. 1, cent deviations, is copied in its entirety and pasted into a third worksheet. The widths of columns A through G will again need to be set at 10. Spreadsheet no. 3, comma distribution, is the same as spreadsheet no. 1 except for the following changes.

Section I Labeling

C3: (blank)
C4: (blank)
E1: "Comma Distribution"

Section I Formulas

D5: =D17/2
D6: =(D11*(10^((702+D43)/3986.3137)))/2
D7: =(D12*(10^((702+D38)/3986.3137)))/2

D8: =(D13*(10^((702+D45)/3986.3137)))/2
D9: =(D14*(10^((702+D40)/3986.3137)))/2
D10: =(D15*(10^((702+D47)/3986.3137)))/2
D11: =(D16*(10^((702+D42)/3986.3137)))/2
D12: =D5*(10^((702+D37)/3986.3137))
D13: =D6*(10^((702+D44)/3986.3137))
D14: 220
D15: =D8*(10^((702+D46)/3986.3137))
D16: =D9*(10^((702+D41)/3986.3137))
D17: =D10*(10^((702+D48)/3986.3137))

Section III Labeling

D35: *"Variable:"*
D36: *"5th Comma"*

As previously mentioned, the spreadsheets are illustrated in figures 13.1, 13.2, and 13.3.

Using the Spreadsheets

Type the name of the temperament in cell B1.

For the cent deviations spreadsheet, insert the values in cells C5 to C16 that represent the cent deviations from equal temperament for the temperament in question. The value for cell C17 would be the same as cell C5. Notice that the notes are listed chromatically (C, C♯, D, E♭, and so on), so the cent values must also be listed chromatically. Once these values are inserted, the values are mirrored in cells E5 to E17.

For the cumulative semitones spreadsheet, insert the values in cells C5 to C17 that represent the cumulative semitones for the temperament in question. With cumulative semitones, the value in cell C5 will always be 0 and the value in cell C17 will always be 1200. As with the cent deviations spreadsheet, the values must be listed chromatically. Once these values are inserted, the values are mirrored in cells F5 to F17.

For the comma distribution spreadsheet, insert the tempering in cents fifths in cells D37 to D48. These are listed according to the circle of fifths (C, G, D, A, and so on). Once these values are inserted, the values are mirrored in cells C37 to C48.

After the values are inserted, all other values will be automatically calculated. Be sure to hit "Enter" after each value is inserted—especially the final entry—to be sure all the calculations are properly carried out. Check to be sure the sum in cell B49 is 8400, the sum in C49 is –24, and the sum in F49 is 4800.

Listings of cent deviations for an assortment of temperaments are available from several sources.[3] Listings of cumulative semitones for an assortment of temperaments may be found in Barbour's *Tuning and Temperament*, available in a recent reprint.

Note that we again encounter the question of precise vs. rounded values. Since entries for cent deviations (cells C5 to C17) and the comma distribution (D37 to D48) are often in terms of rounded-up whole numbers, some of the calculations in the spreadsheets are carried out with rounded-up values for pure fifths (702 instead of 701.9550) and pure major thirds (386 instead of 386.3137). This results in slightly different values for the *c–b* frequencies compared to those given in chapter 12.

	A	B	C	D	E	F	G
1	Name:	Vallotti			Cent Deviations		
2							
3		Equal Temp.	*Variable:*		Cent Dev.	Cumulative	Individual
4	Note	Frequency	*Cent Dev.*	Frequency	from E.T.	Semitones	Semitones
5	c	130.8128	6	131.2669	6	0	0
6	c#	138.5913	0	138.5913	0	94	94
7	d	146.8324	2	147.0021	2	196	102
8	eb	155.5635	4	155.9233	4	298	102
9	e	164.8138	-2	164.6235	-2	392	94
10	f	174.6141	8	175.4229	8	502	110
11	f#	184.9972	-2	184.7836	-2	592	90
12	g	195.9977	4	196.4511	4	698	106
13	g#	207.6523	2	207.8924	2	796	98
14	a	220.0000	0	220.0000	0	894	98
15	bb	233.0819	6	233.8911	6	1000	106
16	b	246.9417	-4	246.3718	-4	1090	90
17	c'	261.6256	6	262.5339	6	1200	110
18							
19		Beat Rates					
20	*Note*	5th	4th	M3rd	m3rd	M6th	
21	c	-0.9	1.2	2.2	-8.0	3.7	
22	c#	0.0	0.0	8.7	8.1	8.7	
23	d	-1.0	1.3	4.1	-4.9	4.1	
24	eb	0.0	0.0	6.2	-11.6	8.0	
25	e	-1.1	1.5	8.5	-5.5	8.4	
26	f	-1.2	0.0	2.9	-13.1	4.9	
27	f#	0.0	0.0	11.6	-8.7	11.6	
28	g	-1.3	1.8	3.2	-9.3	5.5	
29	g#	0.0	0.0	10.7	-15.5	13.1	
30	a	-1.5	2.0	8.7	-7.3	8.7	
31	bb	0.0	0.0	6.6	-17.4	9.3	
32	b	0.0	2.3	15.5	-8.2	15.5	
33	c1	-1.8	2.4	4.3	-16.0	7.3	
34							
35	5th	5th	5th		M3rd	M3rd	M3rd
36	Interval	Cents	Comma		Interval	Cents	Comma
37	C-G	698	-4		C-E	392	6
38	G-D	698	-4		G-B	392	6
39	D-A	698	-4		D-F#	396	10
40	A-E	698	-4		A-C#	400	14
41	E-B	698	-4		E-G#	404	18
42	B-F#	702	0		B-Eb	408	22
43	F#-C#	702	0		F#-Bb	408	22
44	C#-G#	702	0		C#-F	408	22
45	G#-Eb	702	0		G#-C	404	18
46	Eb-Bb	702	0		Eb-G	400	14
47	Bb-F	702	0		Bb-D	396	10
48	F-C	698	-4		F-A	392	6
49		*8400*	*-24*			*4800*	

Figure 13.1. Cent Deviations Spreadsheet

	A	B	C	D	E	F	G
1	Name:	Vallotti			Cumulative Semitones		
2							
3		Equal Temp.	*Variable*		Cent Dev.	Cumulative	Individual
4	Note:	Frequency	*Cumul. ST*	Frequency	from E.T.	Semitones	Semitones
5	c	130.8128	0	131.2669	6.0	0	0
6	c#	138.5913	94	138.5913	0.0	94	94
7	d	146.8324	196	147.0021	2.0	196	102
8	eb	155.5635	298	155.9233	4.0	298	102
9	e	164.8138	392	164.6235	-2.0	392	94
10	f	174.6141	502	175.4229	8.0	502	110
11	f#	184.9972	592	184.7836	-2.0	592	90
12	g	195.9977	698	196.4511	4.0	698	106
13	g#	207.6523	796	207.8924	2.0	796	98
14	a	220.0000	894	220.0000	0.0	894	98
15	bb	233.0819	1000	233.8911	6.0	1000	106
16	b	246.9417	1090	246.3718	-4.0	1090	90
17	c1	261.6256	1200	262.5339	6.0	1200	110
18							
19		Beat Rates					
20	*Note*	5th	4th	M3rd	m3rd	M6th	
21	c	-0.9	1.2	2.2	-8.0	3.7	
22	c#	0.0	0.0	8.7	-8.4	8.7	
23	d	-1.0	1.3	4.1	-4.9	4.1	
24	eb	0.0	0.0	6.2	-11.6	8.0	
25	e	-1.1	1.5	8.5	-5.5	8.4	
26	f	-1.2	0.0	2.9	-13.1	4.9	
27	f#	0.0	0.0	11.6	-8.7	11.6	
28	g	-1.3	1.8	3.2	-9.3	5.5	
29	g#	0.0	0.0	10.7	-15.5	13.1	
30	a	-1.5	2.0	8.7	-7.3	8.7	
31	bb	0.0	0.0	6.6	-17.4	9.3	
32	b	0.0	2.3	15.5	-8.2	15.5	
33	c1	-1.8	2.4	4.3	-16.0	7.3	
34							
35	5th	5th	5th		M3rd	M3rd	M3rd
36	Interval	Cents	Comma		Interval	Cents	Comma
37	C-G	698	-4		C-E	392	6
38	G-D	698	-4		G-B	392	6
39	D-A	698	-4		D-F#	396	10
40	A-E	698	-4		A-C#	400	14
41	E-B	698	-4		E-G#	404	18
42	B-F#	702	0		B-Eb	408	22
43	F#-C#	702	0		F#-Bb	408	22
44	C#-G#	702	0		C#-F	408	22
45	G#-Eb	702	0		G#-C	404	18
46	Eb-Bb	702	0		Eb-G	400	14
47	Bb-F	702	0		Bb-D	396	10
48	F-C	698	-4		F-A	392	6
49		*8400*	*-24*			*4800*	

Figure 13.2. Cumulative Semitones Spreadsheet

	A	B	C	D	E	F	G
1	Name:	Vallotti			Comma Distribution		
2							
3		Equal Temp.			Cent Dev.	Cumulative	Individual
4	Note:	Frequency		Frequency	from E.T.	Semitones	Semitones
5	c	130.8128		131.2669	6.0	0	0
6	c#	138.5913		138.5913	0.0	94	94
7	d	146.8324		147.0021	2.0	196	102
8	eb	155.5635		155.9233	4.0	298	102
9	e	164.8138		164.6235	-2.0	392	94
10	f	174.6141		175.4229	8.0	502	110
11	f#	184.9972		184.7836	-2.0	592	90
12	g	195.9977		196.4511	4.0	698	106
13	g#	207.6523		207.8924	2.0	796	98
14	a	220.0000		220.0000	0.0	894	98
15	bb	233.0819		233.8911	6.0	1000	106
16	b	246.9417		246.3718	-4.0	1090	90
17	c1	261.6256		262.5339	6.0	1200	110
18							
19		Beat Rates					
20	Note	5th	4th	M3rd	m3rd	M6th	
21	c	-0.9	1.2	2.2	-8.0	3.7	
22	c#	0.0	0.0	8.7	-8.4	8.7	
23	d	-1.0	1.3	4.1	-4.9	4.1	
24	eb	0.0	0.0	6.2	-11.6	8.0	
25	e	-1.1	1.5	8.5	-5.5	8.4	
26	f	-1.2	0.0	2.9	-13.1	4.9	
27	f#	0.0	0.0	11.6	-8.7	11.6	
28	g	-1.3	1.8	3.2	-9.3	5.5	
29	g#	0.0	0.0	10.7	-15.5	13.1	
30	a	-1.5	2.0	8.7	-7.3	8.7	
31	bb	0.0	0.0	6.6	-17.4	9.3	
32	b	0.0	2.3	15.5	-8.2	15.5	
33	c1	-1.8	2.4	4.3	-16.0	7.3	
34							
35	5th	5th	5th	*Variable:*	M3rd	M3rd	M3rd
36	Interval	Cents	Comma	*5th Comma*	Interval	Cents	Comma
37	C-G	698	-4	-4	C-E	392	6
38	G-D	698	-4	-4	G-B	392	6
39	D-A	698	-4	-4	D-F#	396	10
40	A-E	698	-4	-4	A-C#	400	14
41	E-B	698	-4	-4	E-G#	404	18
42	B-F#	702	0	0	B-Eb	408	22
43	F#-C#	702	0	0	F#-Bb	408	22
44	C#-G#	702	0	0	C#-F	408	22
45	G#-Eb	702	0	0	G#-C	404	18
46	Eb-Bb	702	0	0	Eb-G	400	14
47	Bb-F	702	0	0	Bb-D	396	10
48	F-C	698	-4	-4	F-A	392	6
49		*8400*	*-24*			*4800*	

Figure 13.3. Comma Distribution Spreadsheet

Notes

1. Owen Jorgensen, *Tuning: Containing the Perfection of Eighteenth-Century Temperament, the Lost Art of Nineteenth-Century Temperament, and the Science of Equal Temperament, Complete with Instructions for Aural and Electronic Tuning* (East Lansing: Michigan State University Press, 1991).

2. J. Murray Barbour, *Tuning and Temperament: A Historical Survey* (East Lansing: Michigan State College Press, 1951. Reprint New York: DaCapo Press, 1972. Reprint Mineola, N.Y.: Dover Publications, 2004).

3. Barbour, *Tuning and Temperament*; Claviers Baroques, "Schedule for Tuning Various Temperaments Using an Electronic Tuner with Meter," 2004, http://www.claviersbaroques.com/CBExpertTemperamentsWithMeter.htm (22 November 2004); Instrument-Tuner, "Temperaments of Instrument-Tuner," 2004, http://www.instrument-tuner.com/temperaments.html (18 October 2004); Jorgensen, *Tuning*; and Paul Poletti, "Temperaments for Dummies," 2001/2003, http://www.polettipiano.com/Media/T4D.PDF (9 September 2003).

14

Instructions in Musical Notation

The following figures (14.1–14.18) display the written instructions from chapter 6 in musical notation, which may be used as a concise, alternate summary once the complete instructions are understood. This type of format has been used by Jorgensen, Klop, and Tittle.[1]

A half note represents the pitch in the interval that is tuned. Beat rates are given above the interval, with a plus sign denoting an interval wider than pure and a minus sign denoting an interval narrower than pure. Pure intervals are so labeled. The simple equal sign "=" is used when the beat rates of two intervals are exactly the same, and the parenthetical equal sign "(=)" is used when the beat rates are similar but slightly different. The less-than sign "<" is used when the first of two beat rates is less than a second beat rate.

Figure 14.1. Pythagorean Tuning

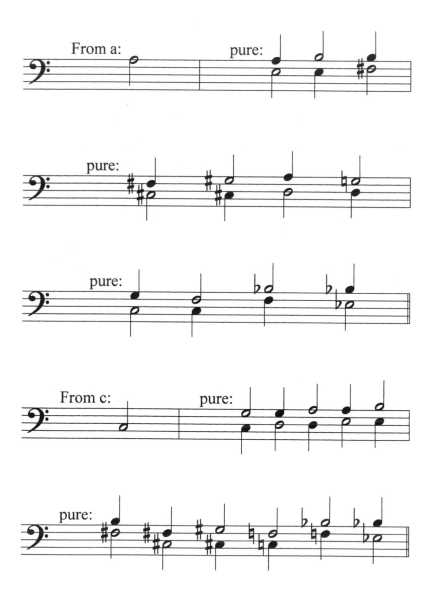

Figure 14.2. 1/4-Comma Meantone Temperament

Figure 14.3. Werckmeister III

Figure 14.4. Kirnberger III

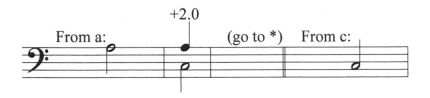

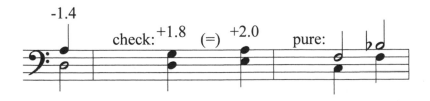

Figure 14.5. Vallotti

Figure 14.6. Young No. 2

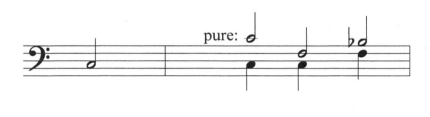

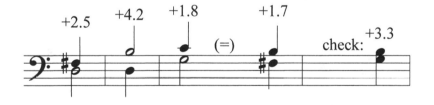

Figure 14.7. Neidhardt Circulating Temperament No. 1

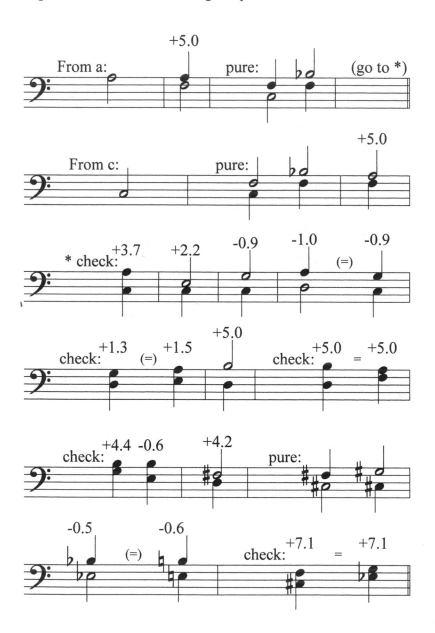

Figure 14.8. *Tempérament Ordinaire*

Figure 14.9. 1/6-Comma Meantone Temperament

Figure 14.10. Rameau

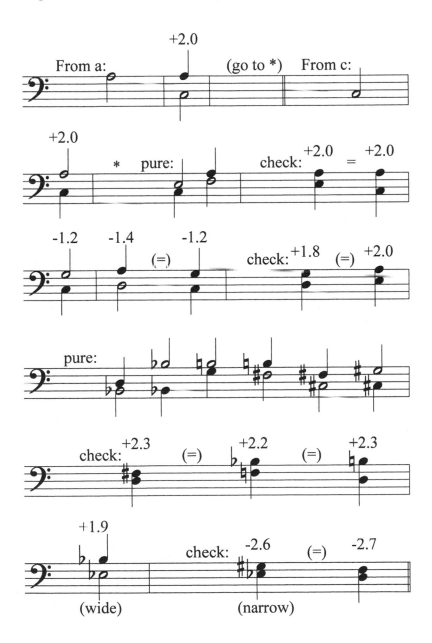

Figure 14.11. Sorge

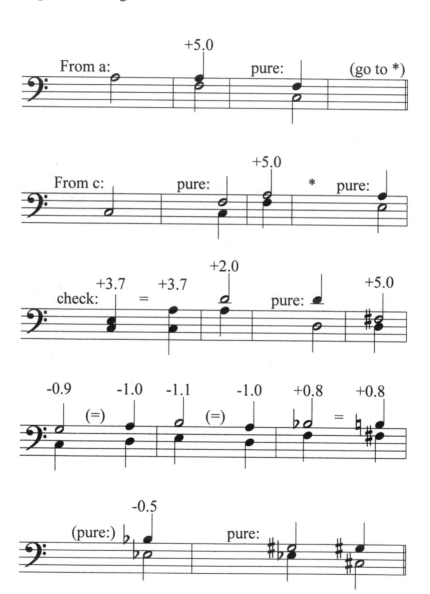

Figure 14.12. Young No. 1

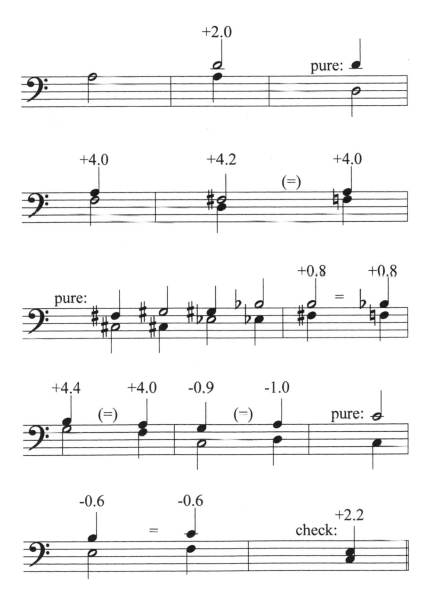

Figure 14.13. Kellner

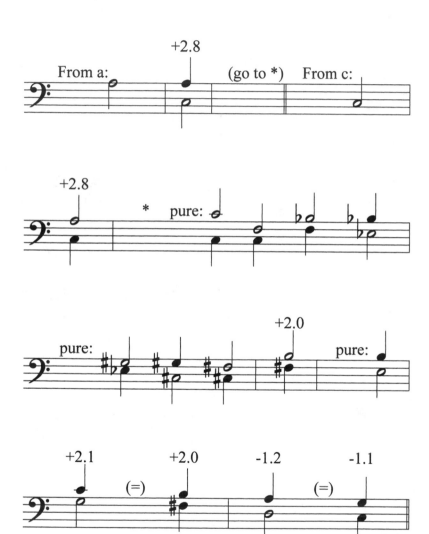

Figure 14.14. Barnes

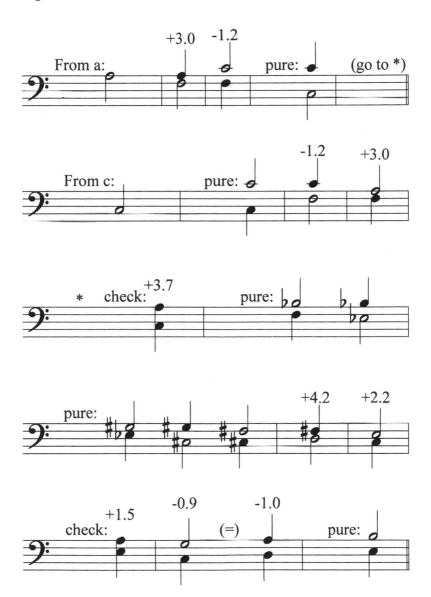

Figure 14.15. Lindley

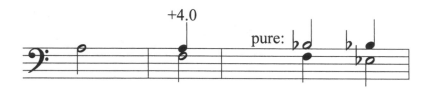

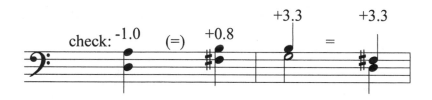

Figure 14.16. Equal Temperament

Figure 14.17. Near-Equal Temperament, from *a*

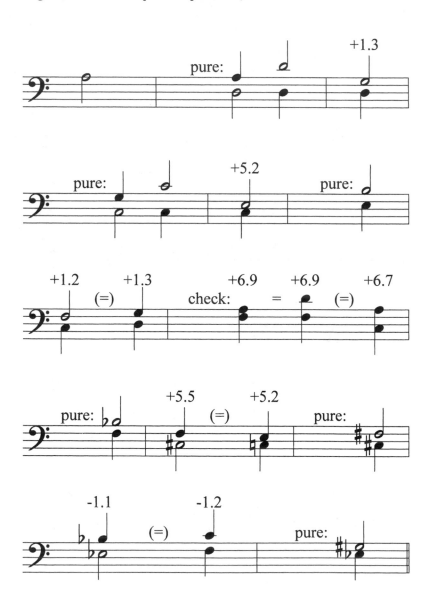

Figure 14.18. Near-Equal Temperament, from *c*

Note

1. Owen Jorgensen, *Tuning: Containing the Perfection of Eighteenth-Century Temperament, the Lost Art of Nineteenth-Century Temperament, and the Science of Equal Temperament, Complete with Instructions for Aural and Electronic Tuning* (East Lansing: Michigan State University Press, 1991); Owen Jorgensen, *The Equal-Beating Temperaments*, 2nd ed. (Hendersonville, N.C.: Sunbury Press, 2000); G. C. Klop, *Harpsichord Tuning*, trans. Glen Wilson (Garderen, Holland: Werkplaats voor Clavecimbelbouw, 1974. Reprint, 1983); and Martin B. Tittle, *A Performer's Guide through Historical Keyboard Tunings*, rev. ed. (Ann Arbor, Mich.: Anderson Press, 1987).

Glossary

The following definitions are not meant to be complete, in-depth definitions of the selected musical terms. Rather, they are specifically designed to explain the terms with respect to the subject of temperament.

A392. A pitch reference or standard in which the A above middle C (a^l) has a frequency that is two equal-tempered semitones below 440 Hz; that is, 391.9954 Hz.

A415. A pitch reference or standard in which the A above middle C (a^l) has a frequency that is one equal-tempered semitone below 440 Hz; that is, 415.3047 Hz.

A440. A pitch reference or standard in which the A above middle C (a^l) has a frequency of 440 Hz.

bearing octave. The region of the keyboard where one tunes and tempers a series of intervals so that the notes of the chromatic scale are properly adjusted in pitch according to a temperament plan. The bearing octave is usually at or near the tenor octave in a keyboard instrument.

beat rate. The number of beats per second of a tempered (non-pure) interval.

beats. The wavering or fluctuating effect that occurs between tones with slightly different frequencies. In tempered (non-pure) intervals, beats are caused by the difference between coinciding harmonic frequencies.

cents. A number that can be used to characterize the size of an interval, based on the logarithm of the frequency ratio. One cent is 1/100 of an equal-tempered semitone, so there are 1200 cents in an octave.

chromatic scale. See **scale**.

chromatic semitone. See **semitone**.

circle of fifths. An arrangement of the twelve notes in the chromatic scale so that adjacent note names describe the interval of a fifth: C, G, D, A, E, B, F♯, C♯, G♯, E♭, B♭, and F.

circulating temperament. See **temperament**.

coinciding harmonic frequencies. Two upper harmonic frequencies, one from each note in an interval, that have exactly the same value when an interval is pure and have slightly different values when an interval is not pure. The numbers in the frequency ratio of the interval identify which harmonic frequencies are the coinciding ones. The difference between the coinciding harmonic frequencies causes beats.

comma. A tuning discrepancy.

> **Pythagorean (ditonic) c.** The discrepancy between twelve pure fifths and seven pure octaves. It is approximately 24 cents.
>
> **syntonic c.** The discrepancy between a Pythagorean third and a pure major third. It is approximately 22 cents.

complex sound. A sound that is composed of several constituent parts or partial sounds. The opposite of a complex sound is a simple sound such as a sine wave.

diatonic scale. See **scale**.

diatonic semitone. See **semitone**.

dominant. Refers to the fifth note in a major or minor diatonic scale. In the key of C major, G is the dominant note, and G–B–D is the dominant triad.

enharmonic notes. Notes that are spelled differently but represent the same sound or pitch, such as D♯ and E♭ in equal temperament. Enharmonic notes exist in equal temperament and in the well-tempered systems, but not in meantone temperament.

equal-beating. Refers to a method of setting a temperament in which two tempered intervals are made to beat at the same rate, even though this deviates from the mathematically strict beat rates. Contrast **theoretically correct**.

equal temperament. A plan in which the Pythagorean comma is distributed equally among the twelve intervals in the circle of fifths; that is, each fifth in the circle of fifths is tempered by one-twelfth of the Pythagorean comma. All fifths are of equal size (700 cents), all thirds are of equal size (400 cents), and all semitones are of equal size (100 cents).

equal-tempered semitone. See **semitone**.

fifth. An interval whose two notes are the first and fifth degrees of a diatonic scale; for example, C–D–E–F–**G**–A–B. A pure perfect fifth has a frequency ratio of 3:2 and a value of 702 cents.

fixed intonation. The characteristic of keyboard instruments that does not allow adjustment of the pitch as one performs.

fourth. An interval whose two notes are the first and fourth degrees of a diatonic scale—for example, C–D–E–**F**–G–A–B. A pure perfect fourth has a frequency ratio of 4:3 and a value of 498 cents.

frequency. The number of periodic vibrations in a musical tone in cycles per second.

frequency ratio. The relationship of the frequencies of the two notes in an interval. Pure intervals have the following frequency ratios: the octave 2:1, the fifth 3:2, the fourth 4:3, the major third 5:4, the minor third 6:5, and the major sixth 5:3.

fundamental frequency. In a musical tone, the lowest partial sound that has periodic vibrations. It corresponds to the note being played.

harmonic frequency, upper. In a musical tone, the partial sounds that have periodic vibrations, with frequencies greater than the fundamental frequency.

harmonic series. The collection of fundamental frequency and upper harmonic frequencies that are related by whole numbers. In general terms: the nth harmonic frequency is n times the fundamental frequency.

Hertz. Cycles per second, abbreviated Hz.

interval. The relationship between two notes or pitches.

irregular temperament. See **temperament.**

just. With respect to intervals, a synonym for **pure.**

just scale, just intonation. A theory of tuning based on pure octaves, pure fifths, and pure major thirds, in which the frequency relationships of the notes are according to small whole numbers (2:1, 3:2, and 5:4) as found in the harmonic series.

laying the bearings. Tuning and tempering a series of intervals after one note is tuned to a standard pitch so that the other eleven notes in the chromatic scale are properly adjusted in pitch according to a temperament plan. This is usually done at or near the tenor octave in a keyboard instrument.

leading tone. The seventh note of a major or minor diatonic scale. In the key of C, B is the leading tone.

meantone temperament. A plan in which eleven of the intervals in the circle of fifths are tempered to the same degree and in such a way that the result is eight pure or near-pure major thirds and a wolf interval. Each of the "good" thirds has a whole tone exactly in the middle, so it is the average or "mean" tone.

modified m. t. A plan that is primarily based on a regular meantone temperament but which is altered to ease the effect of the wolf interval.

octave. An interval whose two notes are the first and eighth degrees of a diatonic scale; for example, C–D–E–F–G–A–B–C. A pure octave has a frequency ratio of 2:1 and a value of 1200 cents.

overtone. In a musical tone, any partial sound "over" (higher than, above) the fundamental frequency. Because of the confusion with numbering (the first overtone is the second harmonic frequency), this term should not be used as a synonym for **upper harmonic frequency.**

partial sound. One of the constituent parts of a complex sound: fundamental frequency, upper harmonic frequencies, and noise.

perfect. Refers to an interval that does not have a major and minor form (as thirds do); perfect intervals include the unison, fourth, fifth, and octave.

periodic. Refers to anything that occurs in a regular manner such as the movement of a clock pendulum or a heartbeat.

pitch. The subjective experience of frequency as it relates to the highness or lowness of a musical tone; generally, the greater the frequency, the greater the perceived pitch. However, the relation of frequency to pitch is not exact; for example, raising the intensity or loudness of a tone causes a rise in pitch even when the frequency remains constant.

pitch level, pitch reference, pitch standard. The association of a note name with a frequency, such as $a^1 = 440$ Hz, especially one that is adopted by consensus.

pure. Refers to the quality of an interval in which the two notes are tuned so there are no beats. Pure intervals have simple frequency ratios.

Pythagorean comma. See **comma.**

Pythagorean third. See **third.**

Pythagorean tuning. A plan in which eleven of the twelve intervals in the circle of fifths are tuned pure.

regular temperament. See **temperament**.

scale. A group of notes or pitches in a certain order.

    chromatic s. A group of twelve notes or pitches within the octave arranged by semitones: C, C♯, D, E♭, E, F, F♯, G, G♯, A B♭, and B.

    diatonic s. A group of seven notes or pitches which follows the arrangement of the natural ("white") keys on the modern piano from C to C; for example: C, D, E, F, G, A, and B.

schisma. The difference between the Pythagorean comma and the syntonic comma. It is approximately 2 cents.

semitone. The smallest interval in traditional Western music, demonstrated by the keys immediately adjacent to each other on the standard keyboard: C–C♯, C♯–D, D–E♭, E♭–E, and so on. There are twelve semitones to the octave.

    chromatic s. Adjacent notes spelled with the same note name, such as C–C♯ or E♭–E. Chromatic semitones are *not* found in a major or minor diatonic scale.

    diatonic s. Adjacent notes spelled with different note names, such as C♯–D or A–B♭. Diatonic semitones are found in diatonic scales, such as D, E, F♯, **G**, A, B, C♯, **D**.

    equal-tempered s. Adjacent notes whose frequencies are related by $2^{1/12}$ (the twelfth root of 2), which is 1.059463094.

sixth. An interval whose two notes are the first and sixth degrees of a diatonic scale; for example, C–D–E–F–G–A–B. Examples are the major sixth (C–A) which when pure has a frequency ratio of 5:3 and a value of 884 cents, and the minor sixth (C–A♭) which when pure has a frequency ratio of 8:5 and a value of 814 cents.

subdominant. Refers to the fourth note in a major or minor diatonic scale. In the key of C major, F is the subdominant note, and F–A–C is the subdominant triad.

syntonic comma. See **comma**.

temper, v. To adjust the size of an interval by making it narrower or wider than pure. Contrast **tune** (2).

temperament. Any plan that describes adjustments to the sizes of some or all of the intervals in the circle of fifths so that they accommodate pure octaves and produce certain sizes of major thirds.

    circulating t. A plan in which one can play in or modulate through all the key signatures since there are no unusable intervals.

    irregular t. A plan in which the fifths are of various sizes, in contrast to a regular temperament such as meantone.

regular t. A plan in which all the fifths are the same size, as in meantone temperament, excluding any wolf interval.

unequal t. A plan in which the fifths are of various sizes, in contrast to equal temperament.

tenor octave. The twelve notes below middle C, denoted by the lower case letters c, $c\sharp$, d, $e\flat$, e, f, $f\sharp$, g, $g\sharp$, a, $b\flat$, and b.

theoretically correct. Refers to a method of setting a temperament in which the tempered intervals closely follow the beat rates of the mathematical representation of the temperament. Contrast **equal-beating**.

third. An interval whose two notes are the first and third degrees of a diatonic scale; for example, C–D–E–F–G–A–B. Examples are the major third (C–E) which when pure has a frequency ratio of 5:4 and a value of 386 cents, and the minor third (C–E$\flat$) which when pure has a frequency ratio of 6:5 and a value of 316 cents.

equal-tempered t. The major third found in equal temperament. Its value is 400 cents.

Pythagorean t. A major third found in Pythagorean tuning that is derived from four pure fifths. Its value is 408 cents.

timbre. The quality of a sound that differentiates one instrument from another, even when notes of the same frequency and loudness are played. It is primarily based on how many upper harmonic frequencies there are and how strong they are.

tone color. See **timbre**.

tonic. Refers to the first note in a major or minor diatonic scale. In the key of C major, C is the tonic note, and C–E–G is the tonic triad.

triad. A collection of three notes or pitches, commonly referred to as a chord.

tune, v. (1) To adjust the pitch of a note to a standard pitch, such as tuning a^l to an A440 tuning fork. (2) To adjust the pitch of one note in an interval so the interval does not beat, such as tuning a pure fifth. Contrast **temper**. (3) The **tuning process**.

tuning fork. A Y-shaped piece of metal that vibrates at a given frequency when struck. It is used as a pitch reference for tuning the first note before laying the bearings.

tuning instructions. A list describing which intervals to tune and temper so that a temperament may be established in the bearing octave of a keyboard instrument.

tuning process. In terms of the stringed keyboard instruments, the sum total of all the steps involved in bringing every string in an instrument to its proper pitch. It includes: selecting a pitch reference, laying the bearings, and tuning other notes to the bearing octave. It is usually referred to simply as "tuning."

unequal temperament. See **temperament**.

unison. (1) The "interval" of a note with itself, most explicit when two notes of the same pitch are placed side-by-side on a musical staff. (2) In a harpsichord, clavichord, or fortepiano, two strings with the same frequency activated by the same key.

upper harmonic frequency. See **harmonic frequency, upper**.

well temperament. This is an objectionable term. See **well-tempered system**.

well-tempered, adj. (1) Appropriately tuned. (2) Having the characteristics of a **well-tempered system**.

well-tempered system. Any plan in which there is no wolf interval and all key signatures are usable.

wolf interval. In a meantone temperament, the excessively wide diminished sixth typically found between G♯ and E♭ that is left over after all other intervals in the circle of fifths have been tempered. It is of limited musical use.

Bibliography

Aaron, Pietro. *Thoscanello de la musica.* Venice, 1523.

Backus, John. *The Acoustical Foundations of Music.* 2nd ed. New York: W. W. Norton & Company, 1977.

Barbour, J. Murray. *Tuning and Temperament: A Historical Survey.* East Lansing: Michigan State College Press, 1951. Reprint, New York: DaCapo Press, 1972. Reprint, Mineola, N.Y.: Dover Publications, 2004.

Barnes, John. "Bach's Keyboard Temperament: Internal Evidence from the *Well-Tempered Clavier*." *Early Music* 7 (April 1979): 236–49.

Deobo, Carey "Resources: Technical Library: Tuning, Temperament." 2003. http:// www.hpschd.nu (12 July 2003).

Blood, William. "'Well-Tempering' the Clavier: Five Methods." *Early Music* 7 (October 1979): 491, 493, 495.

Bond, Ann. *A Guide to the Harpsichord.* Portland, Oreg.: Amadeus Press, 1997.

Briggs, Keith. "Letter to the Editor." *Early Music Review,* May 2003.

Broekaert, Johan. "Harmony and Melody: The Tuning of Classic Music Instrumentation by Means of Objective Pitch Measurement." 2002. http://home.tiscali.be/johan.broekaert3/Tuning_English.html (30 August 2003).

Carr, Dale C. "A Practical Introduction to Unequal Temperament." *Diapason* 65 (February 1974): 6–8.

Cho, Gene Jinsiong. *The Discovery of Musical Equal Temperament in China and Europe in the Sixteenth Century.* Lewiston, N.Y.: Edwin Mellen Press, 2003.

Claviers Baroques. "Schedule for Tuning Various Temperaments Using an Electronic Tuner with Meter." 2004. http://www.claviersbaroques.com/CBExpertTemperamentsWithMeter.htm (22 November 2004).

Di Veroli, Claudio. "Unequal Temperaments." 2003. http://temper
.braybaroque.ie (16 September 2003).

———. *Unequal Temperaments and Their Role in the Performance of Early Music*. Buenos Aires: Artes Gráficas Farro, 1978.

Donahue, Thomas. *The Modern Classical Organ: A Guide to Its Physical and Musical Structure and Performance Implications*. Jefferson, N.C.: McFarland & Company, 1991.

———. "A Transposable Temperament." *Diapason* 89 (March 1998): 12.

Duffin, Ross. "Tuning System Spreadsheets." 2003. http://music.cwru
.edu/duffin/tuning/Rec/default.html (9 September 2003).

Francis, John Charles. "Das Wohltemperirte Clavier: Pitch, Tuning, and Temperament Design." 2005. http://www.bach-cantatas.com/
Articles/Das_Wohltemperirte_Clavier.htm (14 July 2005).

Grönewald, Jürgen. "128 Musikalische Temperaturen im Mikrotonalen Vergleich." n.d. http://www.groenewald-berlin.de/Inhaltsverzeichnis
.htm (3 January 2005).

Haynes, Bruce. "Beyond Temperament: Non-Keyboard Intonation in the 17th and 18th Centuries." *Early Music* 19 (August 1991): 357–81.

———. *A History of Performing Pitch: The Story of "A."* Lanham, Md.: Scarecrow Press, 2002.

Hubbard, Frank. *Harpsichord Regulating and Repairing*. Boston: Tuners Supply, 1963.

Instrument-Tuner. "Temperaments of Instrument-Tuner." 2004. http://
www.instrument-tuner.com/temperaments.html (18 October 2004).

Daniel Jencka, "J. S. Bach's Well-Tempered Clavier Tuning Script: A Proposed 1/18th PC Interpretation." 2005. http://bachtuning.jencka
.com/essay.htm (14 July 2005).

Jorgensen, Owen. *The Equal-Beating Temperaments*. 2nd ed. Hendersonville, N.C.: Sunbury Press, 2000.

———. *Tuning: Containing the Perfection of Eighteenth-Century Temperament, the Lost Art of Nineteenth-Century Temperament, and the Science of Equal Temperament, Complete with Instructions for Aural and Electronic Tuning*. East Lansing: Michigan State University Press, 1991.

———. *Tuning the Historical Temperaments by Ear*. Marquette: Northern Michigan University Press, 1977.

Kanter, Jason. "About Temperaments." 2003. http://www.rollingball .com/TemperamentsFrames.html (1 September 2003).

Kellner, Herbert A. "Instructions for Tuning a Harpsichord 'Wohltemperirt.'" n.d. http://ha.kellner.bei.t-online.de (9 September 2003).

———. *The Tuning of My Harpsichord*. Frankfurt/Main: Verlag Das Musikinstrument, 1980.

Kirnberger, Johann Philipp. *Die Kunst des reinen Satzes in der Musik, II*. Berlin/Königsberg, 1776–1779.

Klop, G. C. *Harpsichord Tuning*. Translated by Glen Wilson. Garderen, Holland: Werkplaats voor Clavecimbelbouw, 1974. Reprint, 1983.

Kottick, Edward L. *The Harpsichord Owner's Guide: A Manual for Buyers and Owners*. Chapel Hill: University of North Carolina Press, 1987.

Lange, Helmut K. H. "Gottfried Silbermann's Organ Tuning: A Contribution to the Manner of Performing Ancient Music." Part I: *ISO Information* 8 (September 1972): 543–56. Part II: *ISO Information* 9 (February 1973): 647–58. Part III: *ISO Information* 10 (November 1973): 721–30.

Ledbetter, David. *Bach's* Well-Tempered Clavier: *The 48 Preludes and Fugues*. New Haven: Yale University Press, 2002.

Lehman, Bradley. "Bach's Extraordinary Temperament: Our Rosetta Stone–1." *Early Music* 33 (February 2005): 3–23.

———. "Johann Sebastian Bach's Tuning." 2005. http://www.larips .com/ (11 February 2005).

———. "Keyboard Temperament Analyzer/Calculator." 2000. http://www-personal.umich.edu/~bpl/temper.html, or http://how .to/tune (18 July 2003).

Lewis, Pierre. "Understanding Temperaments." 1998. http://pages .globetrotter.net/roule/temper.htm (30 June 2003).

Lindley, Mark. "An Historical Survey of Meantone Temperaments to 1620." *Early Keyboard Journal* 8 (1990): 5–31.

———. "Instructions for the Clavier Diversely Tempered." *Early Music* 5 (January 1977): 18–23.

———. "J. S. Bach's Tunings." *Musical Times* 126 (December 1985): 721–26.

———. *Lutes, Viols and Temperament*. Cambridge: Cambridge University Press, 1984.

————. "Some Thoughts Concerning the Effects of Tuning on Selected Musical Works (from Landini to Bach)." *Performance Practice Review* 9 (Spring 1996): 114–21.

————. "Temperaments." 3:540–55 in *The New Grove Dictionary of Musical Instruments*. 3 vols. Edited by Stanley Sadie. London: Macmillan Press, 1984.

————. "Temperaments." 475–77 in *Oxford Composer Companions: J.S. Bach*. Edited by Malcolm Boyd. Oxford: Oxford University Press, 1999.

————. "Tuning and Intonation." 169–85 in *Performance Practice: Music After 1600*. The Norton/Grove Handbooks in Music. Edited by Howard Mayer Brown and Stanley Sadie. New York: W. W. Norton & Company, 1989.

————. "Tuning Renaissance and Baroque Keyboard Instruments: Some Guidelines." *Performance Practice Review* 7 (Spring 1994): 85–92.

————. "Well-Tempered Clavier." 3:847–49 in *The New Grove Dictionary of Musical Instruments*. 3 vols. Edited by Stanley Sadie. London: Macmillan Press, 1984.

McNeil, Michael. "An Analysis Tool for Contemporary and Historical Tunings." *Diapason* 78 (February 1978): 14–16.

Op de Coul, Manuel, Brian McLaren, Franck Jedrzejewski, and Dominique Devie. "Tuning and Temperament Bibliography." 2003. http://www.xs4all.nl/~huygensf/doc/bib.html (7 September 2003).

Poletti, Paul. "Temperaments for Dummies." 2001/2003. http://www.polettipiano.com/Media/T4D.PDF (9 September 2003).

Porter, William. "The Meaning of Mean-Tone Temperament." *The American Organist* 15 (December 1981): 36.

Rameau, Jean-Philippe. *Nouveau système de musique théorique*. Paris, 1726.

Ramos de Pareja, Bartolomeo. *Musica practica*. Bologna, 1482.

Randel, Don Michael, ed. *The Harvard Biographical Dictionary of Music*. Cambridge, Mass.: The Belknap Press of Harvard University Press, 1996.

————, ed. *The New Harvard Dictionary of Music*. Cambridge, Mass.: The Belknap Press of Harvard University Press, 1986.

Rasch, Rudolf. "Does 'Well-Tempered' Mean 'Equal-Tempered'?" 293–310 in *Bach, Handel, Scarlatti: Tercentenary Essays*. Edited by Peter Williams. Cambridge: Cambridge University Press, 1985.

————. "Theory of Helmholtz-Beat Frequencies." *Music Perception* 1 (Spring 1984): 308–322.

Rensch, Richard. "The Kirnberger Temperament and its Effect on Organ Sound." *ISO Information* 12 (April 1974): 831–40.

Sadie, Stanley, ed. *The New Grove Dictionary of Musical Instruments.* 3 vols. London: Macmillan Press, 1984.

Schott, Howard. *Playing the Harpsichord.* New York: St. Martin's Press, 1979.

Schulter, Margo. "Pythagorean Tuning and Medieval Polyphony." 1998. http://www.medieval.org/cmfaq/harmony/pyth.html (27 June 2003).

Sloffer, Phil. "Harpsichord Tuning and Repair." n.d. http://music .indiana.edu/som/piano_repair/temperaments/ (14 July 2003).

Snyder, Kerala J. "Bach and Buxtehude at the Large Organ of St. Mary's in Lübeck." 176–89 in *Charles Brenton Fisk, Organ Builder, Vol. I: Essays in His Honor.* Edited by Fenner Douglass, Owen Jander, and Barbara Owen. Easthampton, Mass.: Westfield Center, 1986.

Sorge, Georg Andreas. *Anweisung zur Stimmung und Temperatur in einem Gespräch.* Hamburg, 1744.

Sparschuh, Andreas. "Stimm-Arithmetik des wohltemperierten Klaviers." *Deutsche Mathematiker Vereinigung Jahrestagung* (Mainz, 1999): 154–55.

Steblin, Rita. *A History of Key Characteristics in the Eighteenth and Nineteenth Centuries.* 2nd ed. Rochester, N.Y.: University of Rochester Press, 2002.

Tartini, Giuseppe. *Trattato di musica secondo la vera scienza dell' armonia.* Padua, 1754.

Taylor, Nigel. "Tuning, Temperament, and Bells." n.d. http://www .kirnberger.fsnet.co.uk (24 August 2003).

Tittle, Martin B. *A Performer's Guide through Historical Keyboard Tunings.* Rev. ed. Ann Arbor, Mich.: Anderson Press, 1987.

Troeger, Richard. *Playing Bach on the Keyboard: A Practical Guide.* Pompton Plains, N.J.: Amadeus Press, 2003.

————. *Technique and Interpretation on the Harpsichord and Clavichord.* Bloomington: Indiana University Press, 1987.

Vallotti, Francesco Antonio. *Della scienza teorica e pratica della moderna musica.* Padua, 1779.

Vogel, Harald. "Tuning and Temperament in the North German School of the Seventeenth and Eighteenth Centuries." 237–65 in *Charles Brenton Fisk, Organ Builder, Vol. I: Essays in His Honor.* Edited by Fenner Douglass, Owen Jander, and Barbara Owen. Easthampton, Mass.: Westfield Center, 1986.

Werckmeister, Andreas. *Musicalisches Temperatur.* Quedlinburg, 1691.

———. *Orgel-Probe.* Frankfurt/Main, 1681.

Williams, Peter. "J. S. Bach's Well-Tempered Clavier: A New Approach. 1." *Early Music* 11 (January 1983): 46–52.

———. *The Organ Music of J. S. Bach, Vol. III: A Background.* Cambridge: Cambridge University Press, 1984.

Wolf, Albrecht. "Graphic Representation and Functional Systematics of Historic Musical Temperaments." *ISO Information* 21 (December 1980): 41–70.

Worsfold, Brian. "English Prosody: Word Stress Databases." n.d. http://www.udl.es/usuaris/m0163949/englpros.htm (21 October 2004).

Young, Thomas. "Outlines of Experiments and Inquiries Respecting Sound and Light." *Philosophical Transactions of the Royal Society of London* 90 (London, 1800): 106–50.

Index

["

About the Author

Thomas Donahue received his D.D.S. degree from the State University of New York at Buffalo in 1979. He studied piano and organ with Frank Newcomb, organ with George Damp, organ and harpsichord with Anthony Newman (State University of New York at Purchase), and harpsichord with Joyce Lindorff (Cornell University). His articles have appeared in both music periodicals and dental journals. He is author of *The Modern Classical Organ* (1991), *Gerhard Brunzema: His Work and His Influence* (Scarecrow, 1998), and *Anthony Newman: Music, Energy, Spirit, Healing* (Scarecrow, 2001). When not playing or writing about harpsichords and pipe organs, he enjoys building and restoring them. He lives in New York with his wife, Jane, and his two daughters, Carolyn and Katie.